MASOCHISTIC NATIONALISM

This book examines the nature of the conflict between right-wing populism and multiculturalism: the West's defining conflict in the modern age. Drawing on a plethora of evidence from politics and culture in the West, it argues that these two positions, while antagonistic on the surface, are in fact similar: nationalism and multiculturalism are two names for one idea, the difference between them being simply a matter of geography; both outlooks have their roots in romanticism, sentimentalism, arrogance and a racist outlook. Rather than defend either approach, this volume urges us to consider the importance of roots and argues for greater consideration of what classical liberalism, socialism and feminism can do to break this impasse in our political thinking, with a concern for equality and concern for solidarity, regardless of cultural practice. As such it will appeal to social and political theorists with interests in political sociology and culture.

Göran Adamson is Associate Professor in Sociology, with a PhD from the London School of Economics (LSE), and the author of *Populist Parties and the Failure of the Elites: The Rise of the Austrian Freedom Party (FPÖ)* and *The Trojan Horse: A Leftist Critique of Multiculturalism in the West*.

Routledge Studies in Political Sociology

Performance Action
The Politics of Art Activism
Paula Serafini

Agonistic Articulations in the 'Creative' City
On New Actors and Activism in Berlin's Cultural Politics
Friederike Landau

Talking Collective Action
A Sequential Analysis of Strategic Planning in Anti-Nuclear Groups
Ole Pütz

Brains, Media and Politics
Generating Neoliberal Subjects
Rodolfo Leyva

The New Demagogues
Religion, Masculinity and the Populist Epoch
Joshua Roose

The Political Attitudes of Divided European Citizens
Public Opinion and Social Inequalities in Comparative and Relational Perspective
Christian Lahusen

The Contentious Politics of Expertise
Experts, Activism and Grassroots Environmentalism
Riccardo Emilio Chesta

Comparing and Contrasting the Impact of the COVID-19 Pandemic in the European Union
Linda Hantrais and Marie-Thérèse Letablier

Masochistic Nationalism
Multicultural Self-Hatred and the Infatuation with the Exotic
Göran Adamson

For a full list of titles in this series, please visit: https://www.routledge.com/sociology/series/RSPS

MASOCHISTIC NATIONALISM

Multicultural Self-Hatred and the Infatuation with the Exotic

Göran Adamson

LONDON AND NEW YORK

First published 2021
by Routledge
2 Park Square, Milton Park, Abingdon, Oxon OX14 4RN

and by Routledge
52 Vanderbilt Avenue, New York, NY 10017

Routledge is an imprint of the Taylor & Francis Group, an informa business

© 2021 Göran Adamson

The right of Göran Adamson to be identified as author of this work
has been asserted by him in accordance with sections 77 and 78 of the
Copyright, Designs and Patents Act 1988.

All rights reserved. No part of this book may be reprinted or reproduced or
utilised in any form or by any electronic, mechanical, or other means, now
known or hereafter invented, including photocopying and recording, or in
any information storage or retrieval system, without permission in writing
from the publishers.

Trademark notice: Product or corporate names may be trademarks or
registered trademarks, and are used only for identification and explanation
without intent to infringe.

British Library Cataloguing-in-Publication Data
A catalogue record for this book is available from the British Library

Library of Congress Cataloging-in-Publication Data
A catalogue record has been requested for this book

ISBN: 978-0-367-44231-6 (hbk)
ISBN: 978-0-367-44233-0 (pbk)
ISBN: 978-1-003-00844-6 (ebk)

Typeset in Bembo Std
by KnowledgeWorks Global Ltd.

Masochism: A sexual predisposition named after Leopold von Sacher-Masoch. The masochist experiences sexual pleasure through pain in a context of sexual dominance.

Masochist Nationalism: A political predisposition where masochism is writ large as a collectivist sentiment. The masochist nationalist experiences political pleasure through self-hatred in a context of political dominance.

To staff and guests at Ras Hotel, Addis Ababa

CONTENTS

Preface	*xi*
Foreword	*xii*
Acknowledgements	*xv*

1	Introduction	1
2	Historical background	3
3	The power of the past	8
4	The virtue of amnesia and the vice of difference	27
5	The purpose of art, well, that's really none of our business	38
6	The ogre of collectivism	47
7	Power and emotions	57
8	On moral show-off and the hidden benefits of self-abasement	63
9	Death cult and the reactionary onslaught in wit	77
10	1789 and the gestures of condescension	84

x Contents

11	Racism	100
12	A liberal way out of nationalist ossification?	120
13	A final word	128

References *129*
Index *135*

PREFACE

In 2016, buses in London and other major cities in England carried a religious message: "Praise Allah." The content of the message had been examined and accepted by the authorities. In the run up to Christmas 2015, Christian groups asked for permission to show an advert featuring the Lord's Prayer in UK cinemas. This request, however, was turned down by DCM – Digital Cinema Media Agency.[1]

Why was the Muslim request accepted, while the Christian request was rejected? From the point of view of the respective faith, the requests were on equal par. The impact by a few hundred buses and a popular movie was most likely similar. Moreover, this was England, where the Christian faith should have the upper hand. The Lord's Prayer, the Reverend Arun Arora at the Church of England remarked, "has been part of everyday life for centuries," and Simon Calvert of the Christian institute expressed concern that, in England, the Christian faith lately "seems to have become persona non grata."[2] When an Express poll asked "Should the Lord's Prayer be banned?" 82 per cent said no.[3] The decision taken by DCM, then, rested on thin popular support.

Why are Western values often derided in the West? What are the mechanisms behind it? And why are values from overseas given special protection? For years, I have been intrigued by these questions, and as a result, I wrote this book.

Göran Adamson

1   80 per cent agree Lord's Prayer SHOULD be screened at cinemas as Richard Dawkins backs ad.
2   "Praise Allah" bus slogans get green light just months after Lord's Prayer ad gets banned.
3   80 per cent agree Lord's Prayer SHOULD be screened at cinemas as Richard Dawkins backs ad.

FOREWORD

Goran Adamson has made a useful contribution to the growing literature on reverse nationalism and majority culture guilt. His concept of masochistic nationalism, the other side of the coin of ethno-nationalism, in which national sentiment is transferred uncritically to other nations or cultures is a powerful force in progressive politics in both Sweden and the UK.

Both countries have a history of domination which perhaps accounts for the unusual strength of inverted nationalism in both of them. And in England's case, paradoxically, the empire seems to have played an important role in inspiring reverse nationalism. English nationalism came to be diluted into something wider—Britishness or even a wider global, cosmopolitan ethic, akin to the spirt of the Roman empire. The famous English charm and bluster, personified by Boris Johnson, are personality traits designed to downplay dominance and thus make it easier to dominate.

This may have made the English, or at least the highly educated, middle class, English, especially susceptible to Adamson's masochistic nationalism, as their sense of a normal, rooted, English nationalism was actively weakened by empire. And this in turn, many decades later, may have contributed to the depth of the cultural divides on national feeling that were revealed by the Brexit vote.

By the first few decades of the 20th-century a significant part of the English educated middle class felt uncomfortable about their historic domination both within the British isles and in the wider empire, and not without reason. But, as Orwell famously observed, a proportion of them found it easy to transfer their national affections elsewhere, particularly to the Soviet Union.

I remember as a young man moving in mainly left-liberal graduate circles in the 1970s and 1980s finding the idea of even moderate national feeling (maybe apart from support for the national football and cricket teams) to be laughably anachronistic. Sophisticated people were post-national but it was interesting to observe how this only applied to England. Indeed, these same English post-nationalists would proudly boast that they had a Scottish or Irish grandparent, from countries whose nationalisms were just fine because less dominant.

In my language of the Anywheres (the mobile and educated) and the Somewheres (the rooted and less well educated), the Anywheres tend to have weaker group identities than the Somewheres. The Anywheres have, instead, *achieved identities* based on individual educational and professional success and often see attachments to place and group and nation as regressive. But it is only the more extreme Anywheres, the people I call global villagers, who have a more universalist outlook and actively shun national identity. Most Anywheres do identify as British even if not very enthusiastically.

The way people think about racism follows a similar trajectory. Most Somewhere small-c conservatives and centrists think that racism is foolish and unfair but define it as about feeling hostility to or superiority towards a minority outgroup. Liberal Anywheres obviously agree with that definition but they add another element to the definition of racism: too strong an attachment to your own group or nation, from which flow many of the supposed biases that hold back minorities. It is, of course, possible to have too strong an attachment to your own group, that is why we have race discrimination rules to make sure that people don't only hire people from their own group or rent their houses to them and so on.

But the idea of benign forms of majority group attachment—like a decent, moderate nationalism that feels a solidarity with fellow citizens but no hostility to other nations or peoples—is something that many progressives struggle with.

And of course the negation of any attachment to your own ethnic group or national identity often then mutates, as Adamson describes like Orwell before him, into a neurotic attachment to the "other" instead. It is noticeable that the people most concerned about white privilege tend to be privileged whites. Yet as Barack Obama put it: "Most working-class and middle-class white Americans don't feel that they have been particularly privileged by their race."

If you go to a dinner party amongst the educated classes of Dublin or Edinburgh or Cardiff, you would not find a shyness about national identity but you would in London or Oxford or Cambridge. Of course the difference, as I mentioned above, is that England has been a dominant nation. But it is my hope that as sociocultural themes continue to become more central to politics the squeamishness about national identity will come to seem rather silly, masochistic nationalism even more so. It will be more widely acknowledged even among progressives that there can be benign national feelings, that national attachments are helpful for fostering solidarity across classes and for integrating minorities, and that national attachment is no longer about superiority. Specialness but not superiority.

xiv Foreword

Guilt, especially elite guilt, has played an important, and surprisingly unexamined, part in modern history in, among other things, helping to delegitimise both of the ancien regimes prior to the French and Russian revolutions. Guilt can be a positive force but it can also be a damaging and neurotic one that contributes to a shallow gesture politics and widens further the class divide in our educationally stratified societies.

Consider this routine statement of anti-racist political activism: "We must be clear in the workplace that racism and inequality are enemies we must keep fighting; that racism takes many forms; that privilege takes many forms. It's why the Black Lives Matter movement is so important. And that it's not enough to be passively anti-racist; we must take a stand, and we must take action."

And then consider the fact that it was written at the height of the BLM protests by Richard Heaton, the permanent secretary in the Ministry of Justice in the UK. A more establishment position is hard to imagine. BLM is a broad movement without much by way of programme or hierarchy but to the extent that it has a manifesto it calls for the de-funding of the police and its retreat from black communities (the opposite of what most of those communities want).

The anxiety of privileged whites was also captured by the BBC's Andrew Marr on his Sunday programme asking black British historian David Olusoga to tell him: "What should white people be doing to change our lives... to make this a better country for black people." Olusoga didn't really have an answer but talked about the subtle ways that black people are psychologically damaged by systemic racism, in language for example.

Marr's instinct is a perfectly decent one but it reinforces the general assumption that whites are the central problem – which ends up placing too much focus on the white conscience, with even some suggestion of white people asking for absolution from black people.

And I worry that these debates are being heard very differently in white middle England. There is a danger in the UK, and probably in Sweden too, that the different reactions to BLM will drive an even bigger wedge between a progressive establishment, happy to embrace much of the BLM perspective, and the bulk of non-privileged, non-guilty, whites, who are not taking the hiring or promotion decisions that might disadvantage black people, and resent being labelled as racists. This can only strengthen the forces of populism and maybe even extremism.

It is, therefore, important to understand these trends. The inversion and corruption of normal feelings of attachment to place, group and nation, is one of the big psychological factors behind the emergence of "woke" politics in recent years and Goran Adamson has provided a timely guide to it.

David Goodhart
Author of The Road to Somewhere: The New Tribes Shaping British Politics

ACKNOWLEDGEMENTS

This book owes a lot to many people. The waiters at the terrace at Ras Hotel, Addis Ababa, serving the best coffee I have ever tasted. In 2013, Peter Baehr at Lingnan University, Hong Kong, generously provided me an opportunity to present an early manuscript. The following friends and colleagues offered countless advice and suggestions for improvements: Per Brinkemo, Rasmus Dahlstedt, Torben Bech Dyrberg, Jonathan Friedman, Kajsa Friedman, Birgithe Kosevic, Patrick Lindén, Louise Molander, Terri Murray, Mehmet Ümit Necef, Henrik Nilsson, Magnus Norell, Andreas Olsson, Daniel Rauhut, Flemming Rose, Tino Sandadaji, Jan Sjöö, Jens Sörensen, Yehudi O. Webster, and many others.

As a result of suggestions by my editor Neil Jordan, the manuscript was greatly improved. Thanks Neil!

My final debt goes to my wife, Michaela. If any idea managed to pass the acid test of an average dinner conversation with her, it was basically ready for print.

Göran Adamson
Amman, Jordan
14 September, 2020

1

INTRODUCTION

The concept of nationalism is generally seen as an uncalled for defence of the culture and history of one's own nation.[1] As such, it is linked to an intense interest in this nation – its history, cultural expression and general particulars – and to a limited knowledge of and interest in other nations. Its perception of the nation is emotionally charged, and the worldview is sentimental and pessimistic.

There is, however, another and seemingly very different form of nationalism. While an advocate of the previous form would say: "We are the best, and all the others are inferior," the supporter of this other form of nationalism claims: "We should be cautious in passing judgments on others, until we have come to terms with our own severe injustices." Even if these self-critical nationalists rarely declare we are the worst of the lot, they would still conclude we are *no better* than others and at any rate more superficial and less interesting. "We simply have no right to sit on our high horses," and to support their case, they bring up discrimination against women and minorities. One's own nation is not, under this form of nationalism, an object of unswerving defence, but one of relentless attack. Self-aggrandisement has been replaced by self-accusation.

One may argue that this latter idea is the opposite of a self-righteous nationalism. The respective advocates could not disagree more, and while one is a self-proclaimed rightist, the other one is a leftist, or at least claims to be. The antagonism between these two world-views defines the current political discussion. But under the surface similarities abound, the self-critical nationalist is also energetically preoccupied with his own nation. His view of the nation is also based on strong sentiments and a dark, sentimental outlook of the world. While self-righteousness and self-criticism are square opposites, they both emanate from the same basket of concepts, views and sentiments, as they are both the outcome of unchecked emotions. On either side, their respective supporters are surrounded by like-minded, and so their views become increasingly brash and

2 Introduction

hollow. Passionate advocacy of one's own nation, and intense criticism against it are two manifestations of one idea.

Self-critical nationalism has a peculiar side-taste. Normally, a sense of inferiority is not infused by other emotions. It is simply dull and painful, and associated with regret or shame. But this particular self-criticism has a different origin. It is linked to a sense of wellbeing. It is a form of collectivist pain associated with pleasure. Underneath this self-critical nationalism lies not a sense of shame, but of pride and snobbishness. This paradoxical self-importance and pleasure could not exist in case the shortcomings were real. A nation plagued by famine or corruption has no time to boast about it. Instead, this pleasure in pain reveals that the pain is not based on social realities but is purely fabricated. Self-critical nationalism can only occur in wealthy societies.

It is an odd fruit among those who are troubled by the fact that they are privileged and fortunate.

Note

1 The term "nationalism" is a rather vague concept ranging from "civic," liberal nationalism, to nationalism based on "ethnicity." or even, during the Nazi epoch, skin colour. For an overview of various forms of conservatisms and nationalisms, see Pfahl-Traughber, 1994.

Many, however, are deeply attached to their country, even though they would never try to force these nationalist views on others. These emotions were embraced by George Orwell himself, although he called it patriotism (Orwell, 1945). The kind of nationalism discussed here, however, is somewhat more radical. An inward and tolerant attitude of live-and-let-live has been replaced by certain self-righteousness, proselytising, and an obsession with hierarchies, whether this attitude is attached on one's own country or a country overseas.

2

HISTORICAL BACKGROUND

The discussion about various forms of nationalism is not new. A classic critique can be found in George Orwell's *Notes on nationalism* from 1945. "A nationalist," he says, is one who thinks solely, or mainly, in terms of competitive prestige. He may be a "positive" or a "negative" nationalist – that is, he may use his mental energy either in boosting or in denigrating – but at any rate his thoughts always turn on victories, defeats, triumphs and humiliations.[1] Similar sentiments emerge from opposite corners. "All nationalists," Orwell continues, "have the power of not seeing resemblances between similar sets of facts. A British Tory will defend self-determination in Europe and oppose it in India with no feeling of inconsistency." A negative nationalist, on the other hand, will favour nationalist movements in India and oppose them in Europe with no sense of contradiction. "Actions," Orwell maintains, "are held to be good or bad, not on their own merit, but according to who does them." On the part of the country where he has sunk his personality, every "nationalist is capable of the most flagrant dishonesty, but he is also – since he is conscious of serving something bigger than himself – unshakeably certain of being in the right."[2] Whether positive or negative, any form of nationalist will, says Orwell, "claim superiority of the language, the physical beauty of the inhabitants, and perhaps even in climate, scenery and cooking."[3] Orwell's positive and negative nationalist could not disagree more. But they still share a deeper obsession with hierarchies – who is better and who is worse. Orwell describes "Anglophobia," the British version of negative nationalism, in the following manner:

> Within the intelligentsia, a derisive and mildly hostile attitude towards Britain is more or less compulsory, but it is an un-faked emotion in many cases. During the war it was manifested in the defeatism of the intelligentsia, which persisted long after it had become clear that the Axis power

4 Historical background

could not win. Many people were undisguisedly pleased when Singapore fell or when the British were driven out of Greece, and there was a remarkable unwillingness to believe in good news, e.g. al Alamein, or the number of German planes shot down in the battle of Britain.

They were trained to oppose British interests, but still could not embrace Hitler. Therefore, they offered a kind of negation of conservative opinion.

English left-wing intellectuals did not, of course, actually want the Germans or Japanese to win the war, but many of them could not help getting a certain kick out of seeing their own country humiliated, and wanted to feel that the final victory would be due to Russia, or perhaps America, and not to Britain. In foreign politics many intellectuals follow the principle that any faction backed by Britain must be in the wrong. As a result, "enlightened" opinion is quite largely a mirror image of Conservative policy. Anglophobia is always liable to reversal, hence that fairly common spectacle, the pacifist of one war who is a bellicist in the next.[4]

Negative nationalism among British intellectuals was not only linked to hostile emotions against England. They also, Orwell claims, got "a certain kick" out of it. Negative nationalism combines collectivist self-abuse with excitement. It is not the mark of the downtrodden but of the superior.[5] In *Notes on Nationalism* Orwell adds another concept. He calls it "transferred nationalism." While negative nationalism does not require any positive object of loyalty – such as in "Trotskyists who have become simply enemies of the USSR without developing a corresponding loyalty to any other unit," transferred nationalism has gone overseas; it is a form of nationalist allegiance "fastened up on some foreign country."[6] Familiar nationalist sentiments have found a less politically suspect point of reference. It is a kind of Shang-ri-la, Utopia and Eldorado – an object of intense romanticism for a certain Western mind-set. The difference is merely geographical: it is simply *there*, not *here*. For more than a century, Orwell continues, "transferred nationalism has been a common phenomenon among literary intellectuals."[7]

Transferred nationalism is like negative, self-critical nationalism and in addition a positive point of cultural reference. Today, a negative and hostile attitude towards one's own nation only rarely comes "without any positive object of loyalty." Those who hold their own country in low esteem also tend to embrace a positive object of loyalty overseas.[8] Therefore, negative and transferred nationalism may be combined. I propose to call this combination "masochist nationalism."

Masochist nationalism may be separated into five aspects:

1. Hostility towards one's own nation.
2. Self-inflicted pain with no basis in reality.
3. This pain is infused with a sense of pleasure and grandeur.
4. Nationalist sentiments are curtailed only to be unpacked later on behalf of a nation overseas.
5. Loyalty towards another nation as a mirror image of positive nationalism.

Who is a masochist nationalist? To try to illustrate this, we shall return to the citation at the beginning of the chapter, where a Dutch UN Program Officer once said: "Dutch politics, oh, it's so bloody uninteresting!" Why does he say this? Because he thinks nothing is happening politically in Holland. After perhaps 20 years in a country where the UN is needed, politics, to him, is "interesting" when everything is constantly in the balance, when there is a state of emergency, and so on. The Program Officer has acquired a taste for political turmoil, and this taste translates into his preferred image of interesting politics. In this sense, Dutch politics is of course uninteresting because it is uneventful. But this is not necessarily a bad thing. Couldn't you say Dutch politics is uninteresting because it works? Violence and coups have been replaced by calm, efficient negotiations. And is Dutch politics really uninteresting? Subtle negotiations are complicated and very interesting, under the surface at least. When the UN Program Officer dismisses all those fine-tuned achievements for the benefit, it seems, of social unrest, he not only reveals a taste for the primitive and the exotic, but he is also, at least in part, an anti-intellectual.

This Program Officer, then, idealises an exotic culture, and prefers to live in it rather than in his country of birth. If somebody asks him why he stays there when he does not have to, he says it does not disappear just because you are somewhere else, assuming suffering is always present, and we have no right to escape it. But why shouldn't we when millions of refugees are risking their lives for it? Why not live in comfort if you can? And yet he does seem to escape suffering because he lives in a compound guarded by security and surrounded by nannies, cooks, helpers and gardeners, and socialises very little, if at all, with the locals. He lives the life of a colonialist although it is not labelled as such. Of course, he opposes colonialism. He hates Israel but will be air-lifted to a Tel Aviv hospital in hours. He wants to visit Cambodia, but he does not want to experience it. He finds it extremely fascinating, but not because he knows a lot about it, but because he knows almost nothing. His fascination is a sign of his ignorance. He has left his country of origin without ever arriving anywhere else. Somehow, he knows that his dismissive comments about Dutch politics are not really true. He says it because he, and people like him, take pleasure in holding their native country in low esteem.

Just like other expatriates working for international organizations, this UN Program Officer is a good illustration of a masochist nationalist. He holds a hostile attitude towards his own nation. There is an air of pleasure and excitement around his self-patronising phrase above, and there is little reality behind it – Holland is a prosperous country. He prefers violence to efficiency – a surprising trait for someone employed to reduce poverty. The anti-nationalist character of UN-staff does not convince. He merely saves those curtailed nationalist emotions for an overseas country. His loyalty and identification to his faraway duty station resembles an old-fashioned nationalist's loyalty to Britain.

But there is a confusion here. What happened to the conflict between nationalists and globalists? Between the narrow-minded Trump-voter, and the

6 Historical background

progressive, unprejudiced internationalist open to the world? This is the way the antagonism is generally framed, at least by the liberal left. In 2017, David Goodhart published *The Road to Somewhere – The New Tribes Shaping British Politics*, where he along those lines suggests a fundamental contrast between the rooted social conservatives called the "Somewheres," and the rootless "Anywheres" with no national allegiances at all.[9] George Orwell, however, has a slightly different opinion. In fact, the theatrical and vacuous nature of those internationalists is an ingrained part of his entire analysis. These "Anywheres" might give the appearance of real internationalists, and also believe in it themselves. But people who pretend to be unprejudiced, open-minded globalisers, Orwell maintains, are mostly emotionally attached to a foreign culture. Their dismissive attitude towards their own country and civilization tends to come together with a "positive object of loyalty" elsewhere.[10]

The coming discussion will support Orwell's idea. If we can draw any general conclusions based on the limited selection of politicians, academics, journalists and expatriates appearing below, those true globalists and "Anywheres" are very rare in practice. Rather, the major political conflict of our time is between positive nationalists and "masochist nationalists," who have replaced adulation for their own country with the patron's warm emotions for an overseas culture.

The antagonism between positive nationalists and masochist nationalists is a defining political conflict of our time. The positive nationalists: Donald Trump, Nigel Farage and the Brexiteers, The German *AfD*, *Front National*, the Greek *Golden Dawn* and other extreme right-wingers. The masochist nationalists: The UN, the EU and similar organizations, the Washington elites, *New York Times* and *The Guardian*, the globalists and the multiculturalists taking down the borders of the nation state from the outside and from within, Faculties of Social Sciences, and the left-liberal establishment at large. National craze against colonial craze in a state of perpetual political confrontation. Still, underneath on the level of principles very little is happening. In spirit, masochist nationalists are merely calling out those conservative self-edifying phrases from a distant shore, like a familiar echo from overseas.

Below, this superficial antagonism will be brought to attention. The discussion is divided into 29 themes under 9 chapters. Regardless if we talk about the past, about culture, artistic freedom, death cult, or whether you tip your head up or down as you approach strangers, one manifestation of nationalism is merely mirroring another. The final chapter – "Racism" – brings out a recurring aspect in previous chapters.

The key objective above is to question a highly influential left-wing attack on classic nationalist values. In the final discussion, however, a liberal way out of this nationalist infighting will be suggested. Instead of, for instance, endorsing artistic freedom only when it suits your own political conviction, you must defend any art, and in particular art you oppose. This cautious, but principled liberal approach may offer an exit out of the nationalist impasse, whether it comes in the form of a classic, "positive" nationalist, or as a self-abusive masochist nationalist gazing in anticipation towards the horizon.

This book is not academic in the general sense of it, but rather polemical. It does not chiefly try to convince by means of data but by what is sometimes called "the telling detail" – i.e. a single event illustrating a general tendency.

The core definitions in the discussion are rather vague. "Positive" and "masochist" nationalism sometimes appear to drift towards political mainstream, and sometimes in a more radical direction. They are conscious exaggerations and simplifications illustrating underlying differences. Hopefully, this will not cause confusion.

Many examples are from Sweden, my own country, where tendencies towards collectivist, fictitious self-denigration are perhaps stronger than anywhere else in the World.

Notes

1 Orwell, 1945.
2 Ibid.
3 Ibid.
4 Ibid.
5 A few decades later, Kenneth Minogue maintains that this inverse form of nationalism still chiefly is caused by self-hatred: "The eagerness of the […] establishment to abandon British customs […] reveals the extent to which [this frame of mind] arises less from love of others than from hatred of our own form of life." Minogue, 2005, p. xv.
6 Orwell, 1945; Ibid.
7 Ibid.
8 The qualities of masochist nationalism below is rather similar to the ideology of multiculturalism.
9 Goodhart, 2017.
10 Orwell, 1945.

3

THE POWER OF THE PAST

In this chapter, the effect of the past upon positive nationalism and masochist nationalism will be brought to attention. First, the power of roots will be highlighted, followed by an argument that both forms of nationalism have a similar approach to culture. Then, a different and yet similar attitude towards majestic poetry will be brought to attention. Subsequently, it will be maintained that both manifestations of nationalism share a history writing characterised by kitsch. Finally, we will address a particular kind of history books, common in both camps whereby its "own" culture is subject to idealization.

The power of roots

In the eyes of positive nationalists, the present condition of one's own nation can be historically legitimised. To nationalist Germans during the 1930s, the mounting political tension was caused by the unfair Versailles Treaty, and any action could be justified by it. To Nikolaos Michaloliakos, leader of the Greek Golden Dawn, the country's recent financial crisis was the logical reaction to years of abuse by "alien forces," and in particular by the EU. Other nations are not, however, allowed to take action and blame it on some or other historical victimhood. While our roots run deep and strong, the roots of others are weak, short and pathetic.

Masochist nationalists, on the other hand, have no excuses for their own nation. Its claims are portrayed as imperialist and unfair. Nothing may be justified by their countries' roots. No explanation is accepted. The reason why masochist nationalists engage in their own nation's past is not because they are self-righteous, but because they are critical.

A recent seminar at Malmö University College was entitled: "What is – really – Swedish culture?" The question was rhetorical, i.e. to show that nothing really is, and the panel concluded they had no answer. We have no roots. It is all fake and man-made, all imported, stolen or copied from abroad. At a 2005 conference, Lise Bergh – former Swedish Minister of Integration – was asked: "Is Swedish culture worth preserving?" "Well," Bergh replied, "What is Swedish culture?" and added: "I think I've answered the question."[1] A 2020 SAS advertisement campaign posed the question: "What is truly Scandinavian?" "Absolutely nothing," a seductive female voice announced. "Everything is copied" - our democracy, parental leave, rye bread, midsummer pole, and women's rights. "We take everything on our trips abroad, adjust it a little bit, and *voilà!*" *"It is a uniquely Scandinavian thing," the speaker said while a black man was gobbling up a Danish sausage.* "In a way Scandinavia was brought here, piece by piece" by Turks, Russians, Somalis. "We can't wait to see what wonderful things you'll bring home next," the captivating voice maintained, while white-skinned individuals were hugging people from overseas at Copenhagen Airport. Finally, a black Scandinavian questions one thousand years of development: "We are no better than our Viking ancestors."[2]

As in a mirror image of positive nationalists, masochist nationalists do not belittle roots overseas, but treat them with tremendous respect, because their past is seen as deep and authentic. In 2002, Mona Sahlin, Social Democrat and former Prime Minister candidate, spoke at a meeting for the Turkish youth organisation and their newspaper Euroturk. "I think," she said, "this is in a sense the reason why so many Swedes are so jealous of immigrant groups. You have a culture, an identity, a history, something that binds you together. And what do we have? We have midsummer night and ridiculous stuff like that."[3]

One could treat Sahlin's statement as an isolated absurdity. Her words, however, reflect decades of masochist nationalist discourse within the Swedish political elite. As a consequence of our own xenophile blinders, Wolfgang Kowalsky claims, the troublesome aspects in exotic cultures are overlooked for the benefit of its beauty and multicultural exoticism. The argument is this: "The reason why foreigners are met with such jealousy and hate by the domestic population is because foreigners lead such a tempting alternative way of life." "The lack of realism in such a simplistic interpretation," Kowalsky continues, "can hardly be rivalled."[4] Sahlin's statement was commented by Karen Jespersen, Denmark's former Minister of Integration: "It's hard for cultural self-denial to be more monstrous and horrifying than this."[5]

Harsh sentiments towards our own country are not, however, confined to the left. In November 2006, during a visit to Ronna, an immigrant community outside Stockholm, Swedish Conservative Prime Minister Fredrik Reinfeldt said: "Swedish roots are nothing but barbaric. The rest of the development has come from the outside."[6] Perhaps Reinfeldt sounded independent and critical, but in fact he knew what a positive nationalist would say and gained political bona fide by saying the opposite.

Moving from their own nation to nations overseas, masochist nationalists replace contempt for past traditions and ancestors with admiration without any

10 The power of the past

sense of inner conflict. But this is not possible, because either things are real and authentic here and elsewhere, or they are not. They cannot at once be ephemeral and eternal. Masochist nationalists use double standards. Even though masochist nationalism appears to offer an escape from nationalist oratory about "authentic values" and "eternal truths," it is the same familiar root mysticism only on behalf of cultures overseas. Positive nationalists and masochist nationalists attack and defend, with equal intensity and lack of self-reflection, the idea of deep, cultural roots.

The power of culture

Traditional domestic culture plays an important role for positive nationalists. This is expressed in folk dance, clothing and food. In religion and literature; in the idea that our self-understanding is linked to our language, and the fear that it will be "contaminated" by other languages. "We must," so the saying goes, "keep the language of the inhabitants clean." Masochist nationalists could not disagree more. Literature with a nationalist tendency is "racist." People endorsing masochist nationalism only wear folk clothing at masquerades. They don't know much about domestic cooking and are probably proud of it.

It all seems far away from suffocating excesses in nationalist pride. But this kind of criticism towards native cultural pride rarely rest on a principle. Those who engage in it tend to endorse foreign languages, exotic folk music, exotic nationalist-sentimental poetry and exotic recipes with the same ease as they dismiss their domestic counterparts.

Launched as "full of humour and self-irony," a new food programme went on air on Swedish State Television in early 2010. The name of the program – "The country of brown sauce" – expressed a fashionable attitude towards Swedish cooking. Brown sauce is unrefined, and you mash potatoes with it. The Guardian says: "Brown sauce sales are falling: Has Britain finally come to its senses?" and continues:" It was a product of the British Empire, and should have gone the same way."[7] It is hard to explain such a venomous attitude other than as a display of righteous emotions among like-minded. Would the Guardian – a newspaper with masochist nationalist tendencies – similarly draw parallels between curry and Hindu nationalism? The scenario is rather curious: Brown sauce and potatoes, a stock trade in England, is falling slightly. Then journalists announce "Britain" is no longer insane just because they have started attacking this cheap dish out of political reasons.

Swedish language is not important for integration. Home-language education for migrants, however, is vital. This is a microcosm of the dilemma: Language is not important here but important elsewhere. The only ones who have kept defending Swedish language as a key to self-esteem are The Sweden Democrats – a "neo-fascist party," according to Social Democratic Prime Minister Stefan Löfven. The official status of others' language combined with a dismissive attitude towards Swedish language is a good case of masochist nationalism at work – a mirror image of self-mystification positive nationalist style. Whether a nationalist boasts about his own language or a foreign one, he is caught in a neurotic, mental whirlwind of what counts, and what does not count; what is to be respected and revered, and what is to be derided and laughed at. "All nationalists," George Orwell claims, "consider it a duty to spread their own language to the detriment of rival languages."[8] They can't wait to lecture about the glory of "their" language, and if English or German are historically tainted, they will choose Amharic or Thai. Both positive and masochist nationalists are obsessed with hierarchies, abuses, triumphs and humiliations and their feelings for "their" language always have something obsessive about it.

A man from the Ivory Coast living in Malmö, Sweden kept being asked to cook native food, although he always took take-away. He was a software engineer, but that was culturally uninteresting. The black British TV-host Henry Bosnu was criticised for being excessively "intellectual" and not focus on "real" black concerns such as rap music and football on his BBC talk show. As a result, Bosnu lost his job.[9] Why is it accepted to criticise a black person for not catering for "black concerns," while nobody would say that white people should focus "white concerns" – whatever that is? And why do left-wingers say intellectual issues are of no interest to black people? Obsession with our own culture has been replaced by obsession with cultures overseas along with their happy members unspoilt by Western civilisation.

Of course, people have preferences, and a genuine interest in Balinese culture is no different from any other interest. Still, one cannot help suspecting that many Westerners show fascination for non-Western cultures out of moral reasons because, they assume, it will give them an aura of anti-Western righteousness. While an interest in domestic folk dance is likely to raise eyebrows, a passion for Muslim whirling dervishes fits any dinner conversation.

This suspicion is supported by the fact that the enthusiasm for overseas' cultures tends to fade rather quickly, like those aid projects initiated with great ambition only to be abandoned as soon as something more heartfelt is discovered.[10] Instead of cautiously recognizing non-Western cultural expressions with a blend of hesitant interest and consternation, or even ridicule and boredom the way strangers should feel free to react when confronted with our impenetrable traditions such as eating rotten fish and jumping around trees like frogs in the dead of winter, masochist nationalists rush towards overseas' traditions with a wild enthusiasm. This particular interest is ecstatic, superficial and ephemeral, lacking any serious determination, leaping from one cultural artefact to another. It is a good and sad example of the postmodern cultural supermarket. Still, masochist nationalists believe that a genuine interest and understanding of exotic cultures can exist without historical knowledge and lived tradition. But they are mistaken, because this is Western excitement for the exotic – dry, tense and intellectual. This fascination is often indiscriminate and incapable to distinguish between, for

12 The power of the past

instance, genuine Indian music and Indian music seen as kitsch by the country's own musicians.

Bollywood is another case in point. While not even wild horses could drag Western intellectuals to a domestic movie filled with gender stereotypes and a trivial plot, they are happy to line up in front of dancing youngsters from the Indian subcontinent with, it seems, true enthusiasm. Bollywood, veteran actor Victor Banerjee says, "is degrading women to mere sex objects."[11] This entire Western approach is elitist and embarrassing, sometimes harmful. Still, it defines precisely those who advocate cultural "sensitivity." Why would, moreover, paper-thin "understanding" necessarily indicate respect? Why can't indifference or even ridicule be a sign of respect, because we would then recognize how little we know about deep and refined cultural traditions. We force ourselves to show respect even though we know next to nothing, and this vacuous arousal might partly explain all those dressed down Westerners smiling at any overseas' custom.

Pretending to understand any cultural display is not a sign of tolerance but of self-importance. A Vietnamese would never applaud some remote European cultural practise unless she liked it. She would show respect by not clapping her hands or by politely walking away. Why does the European elite always talk about tolerance, when it always fails? While Bollywood movies are practically unknown to the European masses – who cannot show emotions unless they understand – the elites are sufficiently damaged in spirit in order to laugh or cry out of purely moral reasons.

Two forms of criticism of one's own culture must be held apart. One of them opposes any form of uncalled for nationalism. This criticism is against nationalism as a principle. The other one hails overseas' cultures at the expense of domestic culture behind a cloak of progressive language. In case, says Patrick West, Christmas celebrations are turned into "Winterfest" like in Stoke, mid-England, or "Winter celebrations" - Shropshire west of Birmingham - where any trace of religious-cultural tradition has been carefully peeled off, this would only qualify as political principle if other religions were also dismantled and rephrased in cool scientific language. However, it is often a matter of one-sided humbleness, whereby other religious customs are being promoted at the expense of Christian traditions. This, West maintains, is a case of "cognitive dissonance," i.e. simultaneously carrying contradictory ideas. "Some consistency," he adds, "would be most welcome."[12] Similarly, in order to welcome religious buildings from other cultures in the West, such as Park 51 – a Muslim community centre three blocks away from Ground Zero in New York City – one would hope these endeavours are reciprocal; i.e. that churches can be built in Muslim countries.[13] But this is rarely the case. If projects such as Park 51 are not met with equal generosity, and if this is accepted by Western academics, these are masochist nationalists engaged in a zero-sum game and thrilled by it: Non-Western traditions are fostered at the expense of Western traditions. In early July 2020, Hagia Sofia in Istanbul was turned into a mosque, and the inauguration Friday prayer featured

The power of the past **13**

an ominous sword ceremony while Western editors-in-chief were suspiciously eying one another in what appeared to be a well-rehearsed silence. "What if a Christian preacher had made a similar appearance?" Tomas Avenarius wonders in Süddeutsche Zeitung. "A cry in outrage would have filled the Muslim world."[14] Actions are defended or derided, George Orwell maintains, "not on their own merits, but according to who does them."[15] When the principle goes, so does meritocracy. It is good to be a role model for other countries. But there is a thin line between spearheading pluralism and cultural self-denigration, and masochist nationalists seem oblivious about it. A positive nationalist, in comparison, would do the opposite and yet something similar: Requests by foreign cultures would be dismissed while claims from inside his own culture would be endorsed. They are only two different manifestations of cognitive dissonance.

Christopher Caldwell reaches similar conclusions as Orwell above. This cognitive dissonance, Caldwell claims, is partly caused by ignorance: "Europeans who considered churches houses of stupidity, sexism and superstition (do not) know enough about (other religions) to form a judgment, and (leave) them unmolested." They wipe aside familiar myths but embrace new myths about the noble nature of exotic religions "with a childish credulity."[16] Masochist nationalists do not dismiss nationalist culture, even if they pretend to do so. They are merely anti-domestic, anti-native, anti-us, anti-self, and pro-far away, pro-distant, pro-them, pro-exotic, pro-Islam. The more you know about a culture, as it seems, the less you like it. This connection between knowledge and derision is at odds with the familiar idea whereby knowledge modifies hostile emotions. Similarly, the idea that ignorance fuels excitement instead of scepticism belongs to a romantic, conservative tradition whereby the ignorant disciple is deemed wise while the well-read critic is yet to be informed. Of course, our opinions can be based on anything. But one should note this streak of anti-intellectualism among those I refer to as masochist nationalists.

What does this connection between ignorance and excitement mean in terms of identification and dissociation? Masochist nationalists are common in international organization and they often combine little knowledge with strong positive emotions. While an airbus recently was descending over the vineyards of southern France, one of them proudly announced: Oh, I really can't feel at home in France! France is just my passport country, but in Cambodia, I really feel at home in Cambodia, that's where I belong!" And if you gently ask how this is possible, because they don't speak the language or understand the culture or history of anything, they say it is because people in Cambodia are "so wonderfully kind," a stereotypical phrase much the way you would prefer a dog to a cat. They claim to be intimate with a country overseas even though it is de facto alien to them, and they are also most likely strangers in the eyes of Cambodians.

What would a positive nationalist say? He would say Cambodians – as faceless collective – are "completely unreliable." He would have as little evidence in support of it and keep praising his home country in endless ways. Both masochist

14 The power of the past

and positive nationalists take the liberty to feel very strongly about foreign countries they know very little about. Just like the deeply religious, they combine ignorance and excitement, but the excitement heads off in opposite directions. One rules out any intimacy with Cambodians, while the other one cannot wait for it to happen. Masochist nationalists would claim Cambodian's gentle character is because they have overcome the allure of products, while positive nationalists would claim Cambodian's are unreliable because of "their character." But Cambodians may be kind to Expats out of economic reasons, and they might appreciate a soap if only they can afford it. On the other hand, economic hardship might also push you in the other direction towards criminal behaviour. In this sense, both types of nationalism ignore Marx' insight that your behaviour to a great extent is caused by your economic situation. It also appears as if Marxism and progress, in the eyes of masochist nationalists, has been clouded by the allure of primitivism and an infatuation with the exotic.

On the other side of this religious coin of ignorance and passion it says derision towards the familiar. It is not about strong emotional identification with the unknown but about alienations towards your own life and background. In an article entitled "That's why we Swedes eat such strange food," the author brings up the combination of pizza and white cabbage salad – "you can't find it in any country but Sweden," and "a lot of people would find meat with lingonberry quite absurd."[17]

What does it mean to say that the food in your own country is "strange?" It means you have no connection to it. It is unknown. It is like saying the landscape outside your childhood bedroom is "unfamiliar." Clearly, it is possible to favour, say, Vietnamese food to the food of your own country. You may even say you despise everything you ever had when you grew up. But you can't say it is strange because it is part of your life and always will be whether you like it or not. If you say so, you are not only saying you don't like it but – which is different – that it has no relation to you. Preferences is one thing, knowledge another. If you claim not to have any connection to it even though it has been in front of you your entire childhood, you are just playing that old Orwellian game of left-wing self-abuse.

You could argue, of course, that you merely point out that "a lot of people" might not like meat and lingonberry combined. But the insinuation is clear. Others find it strange, and so we jump on the occasion and desert our country in spirit, and as we do it, we sense that Orwellian "kick" of fictitious self-harassment. While Norwegian food might be strange to Americans, because there are not many Norwegians, it can't be strange to Norwegians unless the world is going completely insane.

This willingness to erase your memory in order to comply to some exterior political ambition leads over to another similarity with the positive nationalist, namely a totalitarian attitude towards your history and, basically, to who you are. While a positive nationalist might consider annihilating his personality for the sake of a far-right desire to demonstrate cultural superiority, masochist

The power of the past **15**

nationalists may consider having his mind sucked dry like a fly in the spider's net if he has reason to believe he will have the opportunity to express cultural inferiority.

It is also interesting to note that the writer's hostile views above towards his own background not only puts it in a bad light. It fades, it seems, into oblivion. He dissociates himself from his own previous existence to the point where he even finds it "strange" which is a whole different thing. Strongly negative political views appears to have the power not only to criticize your past, but to erase it altogether. And if the past can be erased by political views, the past can also be created by ideology. Reality, then, is no longer something we must accept, but the outcome of political pressure. From the vantage point of political power, the leap from criticism to creation opens up for a whole different magnitude of possible measures. These measures were always popular among positive nationalists and fascists in order to exercise totalitarian control over strangers and enemies. Photos could be altered, historical events remade in compliance with the dictates of the day. Now, innocently enough, a masochist nationalist pretends to have no relation to native food – a foretaste of complete mind control over the domestic population where not only the future but also the past is the result of political decision.

It might seem excessive to compare a single, innocuous case of cultural dissociation with historical revisionism. But it is a telling detail indicating a deepening trend among Western elites with a tendency towards chic, collective, manufactured self-loathing. In one field after another, they express dissociation, indifference, or even pretend not to have any relation whatsoever to objects and episodes from their culture and their past – an astonishing suggestion and a kind of history mysticism in reverse replay, the corresponding positive nationalist history mysticism of which is found only in the right-wing abyss.

When it comes to war-time paraphernalia freely available on right-wing websites, such as torpedoes turned into rusty vases, masochist nationalists show no mercy. It is all, from what appears to be a pacifist perspective, violent, appalling, fascist and everything you could expect in our male-chauvinist Trumpian times. But as soon as they enter The Walled off Hotel in Bethlehem on the Palestinian side next to the walls of the Jewish settlements, it appears as if their pacifist persuasion was not so pacifist after all. In the hotel you'll find a variety of Palestinian war-time paraphernalia such as hand grenades filled with soap and army bunk beds for sale, but this time masochist nationalists show no sign of disapproval. Instead, they pick up their cameras visibly excited.

Also, while most inconsistencies in this matter require different objects of veneration such as Muslim dancing dervishes versus Norwegian folk dance, all it takes for a masochist nationalist to turn from disapproving to enthusiastic is to tell him an old hand grenade is not German but Palestinian. And if you can't tell its origin, his face will flicker uneasily because he will not know what it means. It is a hand grenade, you'd say, it kills people. But his approach is not pacifist in relation to objects of war, but political in relation to his own personal

16 The power of the past

preferences – i.e. whether he likes it or not. Faced with pacifism as an idea and a principle, any masochist nationalist trembles from fear. Next to him, a real pacifist would calmly oppose war-time paraphernalia without thinking for a second about its ideological content. This shows the striking emptiness of masochist nationalism. A positive nationalist, on the other hand, would marvel at right-wing war objects, but he would refuse to find anything at the Walled off Hotel appealing in the least. They are merely two manifestations of nationalist self-obsession, and indifference to the bigger picture.

Misapprehensions of majestic poetry

In the ensuing discussion, I will try to show how masochist nationalists, behind a reputation of being "critical" and "on the left," often appear both intellectually thin and curiously upper-class, pushing them into close proximity to positive nationalists. An illustration of this tendency relates to their approach towards literature with a grand, romantic tendency. Here is a classic case, an early 20th century Swedish poem by Carl Snoilsky, count, diplomat and man of letters:

> Black swans
> Black swans, black swans
> sliding as in a funeral procession.
> Searching for the forlorn shimmer of sunken suns
> in the hazy waves of the night.
> Its mighty plume
> dark, as if charred by fire.
> The beak, silenced in bloody purple
> still bears witness of the blaze.
> White swans, tamely in the weed
> cruising for favours and bread
> Set out towards the depths, black swans
> set out, you children of night and passion![18]

Faced with romantic verse like this, how would an academic with a bent towards masochist nationalism react? Most likely through a prism of anti-racism. Now, a sentimental "funeral procession" is tantamount to self-idealization paving the way for expansionist visions. The romantic image of the charred, mighty plume would be ridiculed. To the nationalist insider, we'd be informed, the "blaze" and the battle is political extremism, and black swans heading out towards the darkness is the old war longing covered with a layer or kitschy prose. The poem aims for greatness, and greatness is ambition and aspiration, and a masochist nationalist will not accept it. In the opinion of masochist nationalists groomed in postmodernity, yearning, restlessness and quest for truth is – codified – a call for authoritarianism, and the stamping out of dissent. The black swans are "searching" – they have left the safety of the shallow waters. This is an image of dissatisfaction and doubt, all of it interpreted in darkest terms possible as cultural despair, and from here on, as has been shown by Fritz Stern and others, links to racial purity and national resurgence are all too obvious.[19]

These images are all exciting and masochist nationalists are likely to profit politically as a result of it. But they might be misled by their own quest for moral high ground along with an appetite for scary things. In fact, they may confuse fascism for social criticism. While "sorrow" and pessimism are not politically innocent, they may just as well stand for individualism and intellectualism. Optimism is no guarantee against oppression. On the pictures from the construction of the White See Canal under Gulag, the forced labourers were not told to cry but to smile. Pessimists are often insightful and considerate about social matters. By nature, intellectuals are pessimists. Their optimism might lie elsewhere and hope, Jürgen Habermas says, is not necessarily utopianism. The image of black swans struggling in the mist might as well be a mental battle for originality and uncertainty instead of a desire for violence. Doubt and dissent may signify humanism and lack of conviction rather than that absolute negation of hesitancy – war. As a result of all of these looming political misapprehensions, masochist nationalists may start drifting towards Snoilsky's white swans, and end up as advocates of opportunism, indifference, and mediocracy – the world-view of a bland bourgeoisie drinking coffee while feeding white swans cruising for favours.

When masochist nationalists mistake criticism for fascism, a core idea in politics is fading – fascism as at heart anti-intellectual. Instead, fuelled by postmodern misapprehensions, fascism will come out as intellectual. Political exceptionalism blend with intellectual exceptionalism, and the masochist nationalist seek refuge in the bourgeoisie. The reason why the masochist nationalist attitude often has a side taste of arrogance and privilege is, perhaps, partly caused by this unsettling confusion.

The stakes are high in the political matrix of the masochist nationalist. In case the black swan marred by imperfection and uncertainty is exposed as politically suspect, the only rescue, it seems, is to embrace cult of action and political activism. Masochist nationalists also, then, seem to espouse values bordering on fascism. From a conservative point of view, liberalism merges with socialism, and from a masochist nationalist viewpoint, all criticism is fascism, and all fascism is criticism. This proximity with fascism might come as a surprise for those who define themselves as anti-fascists.

When dissent, masochist nationalists conclude, is a political vice, democracy requires conformity. Conflicts, no matter how civilised, are politically suspect, and democracy is defined by hegemony and groupthink. Debate means conflict, conflict is battle, battle is struggle, and struggle fascism. This is how hegemonic power always argued. The university in the West, at least faculties of social sciences, offer a good illustration of these tendencies towards group think, misapprehensions about majestic poetry, and how debate is seamlessly associated with political extremism.

18 The power of the past

The image of the black swan is that of a creature full of doubt and discontent, and yet active, full of hope. The figure is replete with uncertainty, but also with a quest for perfection and utopia. There are certainly dangers involved. Lethargy was rarely politically suspect, while enthusiasm always should be treated with some care, especially if it is associated with dissatisfaction with current circumstances, i.e. with political pessimism. If political excitement is completely detached from the present, these ideas might be fatal." Anyone," said André Malraux," who is both enthusiastic and pessimistic either is a fascist or will become one."

Still, quest for perfection is not tantamount to perfection. In fact, struggle for it and perfection accomplished might be opposites. "I would gladly," some philosopher said, give my life to anyone who said he was searching for truth, but I would gladly kill him if he said he'd found it." For the sake of societal stability and one's vested interests, it is convenient to muddle the gap between search for truth and truth achieved. Perhaps, this partly explains why postmodernism has been such a success among the elites, and also why masochist nationalists for many decades now have used postmodernity in their attempt to slander any dissent and progress, such as black swans aiming for the uncertainties of the open sea.

The black swan's doubt and determination leads over to another difference as compared to the white swan. The white swan is cruising for favours and bread, trying to please the guests at the seaside tables for the sake of personal gain. The white swan is a salesman in submission. She is selling appreciation, hoping to trade it for food. In the end, self-interest, and, in order to get there, slave-like self-abasement. In this sense, she resembles a popular singer, whose entire performance is an attempt to appease, flirt with but ultimately profit from the audience. Despite the commotion, little is happening from the point of view of creativity. The black swan also has the opportunity to spend her day cruising around the seaside café and awaken the pity of the guests. But she is not playing to the crowd. Instead, she turns inward, becomes inapproachable, trying to find answers beyond her own personal interest. In the end, service to the common good, and, along the way, self-obsession. Her approach resembles the classic pianist with eyes closed, self-consumed, perhaps humming, oblivious of the audience but for the sake, notably, of the greater good of piano music. As a result of masochist nationalist scorn for the black swan, she will not only be tempted to embrace that kind of disconcerting bourgeois hostility towards intellectual curiosity, but also, at least by implication, to embrace popular culture where only the most short-sighted egotist will pass the test of political decency.

Above, I have used a poem by Carl Snoilsky to illustrate masochist nationalists' reactions to certain aspects of Western culture. A number of plain virtues from a less unforgiving angle – curiosity, autonomy, intellectualism, hatred towards conformity, lust for adventures, but also scepticism, the benefits of independent cultural creation and performance, doubt and even, perhaps, anxiety, would now be unmasked as right-wing extremism. The politically exceptional fuse with the intellectually exceptional. These political distortions, furthermore, have repercussions in the opposite corner. If doubt means fascism, certainty – even absolute certainly bordering on absolutism – means" anti-fascism." Silence and lack of discussion means tolerance, emancipation, and democracy. Discussion is curtailed in order to allow for it. Anyone familiar with how the anti-racist camp argues realizes that these connections are not entirely spurious. When curiosity becomes politically tainted, postmodern indifference is "anti-racism." When the adventurous in put in a brown bag, the opinionated kitchen philosopher becomes a beacon of virtue. When braveness is far right-wing, we seek refuge in opportunism. If independence and autonomy are both political suspects, begging and cruising for favours in the weed is an anti-racist endeavour. When struggle is war, ineptitude is progress. When submission to a higher common cause is tainted, we cannot tear down social trust fast enough. When debate blend with social upheaval, peace, prosperity and anti-racism can only be achieved through silence – for any purpose and by any means. The dangers of unorthodoxy will be overcome through conformity. In case a willingness to excel, also in self-defence, is magnified as fascism, "anti-racism" requires self-defeatism, and self-defeatism is the backbone of masochist nationalism.

And what about the positive nationalist? He may approach it from the other end. Enthusiastically, he would embrace Snoilsky's poem and the boldness and destiny of the black swans, but fail to grasp its greatness. Instead, the entire imagery of independence and intellectual curiosity would be trivialised and exploited for sordid right-wing objectives. Autonomy would be drenched in pathetic emotionalism; vigour turned crooked and charged with vengeance. Intellectual curiosity mystified as if the entire endeavour is to marvel at the unknown instead of trying to explain it, and individual achievements blown up and distorted into a glorious collective enterprise. Instead of cutting loose from conformity as such, he would embrace a novel form of it. Discipline, finally, would lose its features of independence and creativity, and be brutally transformed into a tool for domination and mindless dependence.

From opposite corners, positive and masochist nationalists wind up in political romanticism. Neither of them recognizes the benefit of cultural dissent. They both can't wait to tie it to right-wing radicalism – the latter via guilt – by association because their scorn of right-wing radicalism makes them unable to tell it apart from independent inquisition; the former because they love far-right ideology and brutally seek to capitalize on every idea that deviates ever so slightly from the dogmas of political correctness. They are equally fanatical about anything seen as impure from a masochist nationalist perspective – the latter in order to brand it, the former in order to embrace it. While the positive nationalist's primitive cult of dissent pushes him towards totalitarianism, the masochist nationalist is impelled in the very same direction due to his postmodern opportunism and his no less crude dismissal of any dissent – perhaps both eloquent and progressive. As George Orwell said: The racists are bound to come back, next time under the name of "anti-racists."

20 The power of the past

To muddle the political waters was always a temptation among political enthusiasts. But they might easily rock their own foundation, whether they realize it or not. When masochist nationalists criticize the black swans in Snoilsky's poem, as I imagine they indeed would do, they are confusing autonomy and independent inquisition with submission and extremism. As a result, they will be heavily influenced by the image of the white swan, i.e. a bourgeois conformist and opportunist. As I will discuss below, these underlying political mechanisms may partly explain why the world-view of the masochist nationalist often appears to be both colonial and upper-class.

Historical kitsch

Previously it was argued that the masochist nationalist, as a result of this indiscriminate appeal for non-Western music, is unable to distinguish between genuine music and kitsch from the Indian subcontinent. This leads over to the perception of history in positive nationalism and masochist nationalism, because this is in both cases characterised by kitsch.

But what is "kitsch?" According to Mehmet Ümit Necef, it is traditionally associated with "poor, cheap art of mass production, satisfying longings and a desire to give the impression of lavishness." In a wider political context, Necef continues, "nostalgia makes use of certain aesthetic expressions, namely sentimental and romantic clichés about traditional and exotic communities." Necef refers to any experience of pre-modern communities influenced by those clichés as "ethnic kitsch."[20] This nostalgic attitude, he continues, is mostly a middle-class sentiment. Kitsch, then, "takes on the role of a pastime activity within the middle-class." The fact that it is "easily accessible creates, at the same time, relaxation, and can hence be seen as a form of entertainment, and as yet another expression of the spare-time hedonism of the middle-class."[21]

As an illustration of "ethnic kitsch" Necef cites the anthropologist Colin Turnbull, and his description of the Mbutu people in the Congo region of Africa: "The infant was conceived in love and joy, and that it is born, equally wanted and welcome whether it is a girl or boy." Then, Necef brings up Peter Berger, to whom Turnbull engages in "an activity of invidious comparisons: The Mbuti are peaceful; we are violent. They cooperate; we compete. Their society is built on consensus, our on coercive law." Mbuti society is "a model of mutuality;" ours is one of division and segmentation." This, Necef concludes, "is what I call "ethnic kitsch."[22]

Above, we have talked about Necef's notion of "ethnic kitsch," signifying a masochist nationalist fallacy. In the present discussion, however, we shall use the broader "historical kitsch," covering both positive and masochist nationalism. It is worth pointing out that kitschy descriptions of infants along with their tolerant and loving parents may just as easily be applied on the West by positive nationalists. In either case, "kitsch," Necef concludes, can be told apart from science for two reasons. First, it is not about reality, but about one's own rosy projections of it. Second, it is not about reality because the very same kitschy images can be applied on just about any country, including one's own.[23] After these opening comments, we shall now briefly discuss two manifestations of historical kitsch.

In the eyes of the positive nationalist, history is tantamount to a cult of our past along with an aloof fascination for the exotic. At first sight, masochist nationalists avoid historical kitsch. They deride positive nationalists and any claim that our past would be "higher" than the past of distant cultures. Instead, our history is demystified and rather than a great chain of events, it is described as a tumultuous array of poorly connected events. From this perspective, masochist nationalism is anti-kitsch.

But if the masochist nationalist reveals the hollowness of historical kitsch with one hand, he upholds them with the other hand. When the first Gulf war between Kuwait and Iraq was over and a Kuwaiti soldier was seen on Swedish TV kissing his regained land, a Social Democrat made an emotional comment about its past containing thick nationalist overtones. Not long before she had expressed derisive views about Sweden's past. Why, Christopher Caldwell wonders, is "ethnic pride" a virtue and "nationalism" a sickness?[24] If you criticize historical kitsch you must dismiss all forms of it. If you oppose an idea, you can't cherry-pick. Masochist nationalists are not opposed to historical kitsch. They are merely hostile towards nostalgia at home while, as in a case of psychological compensation, they fill the void with a passion for historical myths overseas. While domestic historical kitsch is unthinkable, wide-eyed reverence for exotic traditions is under the radar and they can safely plunge into calls for national awakening, cult of action and self-idealization elsewhere. This is all historical kitsch, but somehow not seen as such.

Writing in 1945, George Orwell sees these tendencies as a large-scale form of transference, where the "transferred nationalist," who had found his Patria somewhere else could go to any extreme without the slightest risk of being caught. Although his nationalist perception had not changed, he could still count on warm greetings wherever he announced his paper-thin internationalism. This opportunity to trade a tainted Britain or Germany for something fresh and afar makes it, Orwell claims, possible "to be much more nationalistic – more vulgar, more silly, more malignant, more dishonest – than he could ever be on behalf of his native country, or any unit of which he had real knowledge."

Orwell continues:

When one sees the slavish or boastful rubbish that is written about Stalin, the Red Army, etc. by fairly intelligent and sensitive people, one realizes that this is only possible because some kind of dislocation has taken place. In societies such as ours, it is unusual for anyone describable as an intellectual to feel a very deep attachment to his own country. Public opinion – that is, the section of public opinion of which he as an intellectual is aware – will not allow him to do so. Most of the people surrounding him are sceptical and disaffected, and he may adopt the same attitude from imitativeness or sheer cowardice(.).[25]

22 The power of the past

The dislocation Orwell talks about among "fairly sensitive people" illustrates the shift from positive nationalism to transferred nationalism within the educated classes. Submissive historical kitsch in honour of our kings is not allowed, but slavish rhetoric about Stalin is accepted.

But how conscious is this masochist nationalist attitude really? Is it only a tactical attempt by a pragmatic nationalist to escape condemnation by that "section of public opinion of which he as an intellectual is aware?" Does he merely choose a foreign historical past in order to be able to unleash his nationalist passions safely, without any political risk involved? Or is his internationalism actually a genuine feeling? If someone argued that he sounds very much like a positive nationalist, would he admit he was merely looking for a way out of political accusations or rather be taken aback by the mere comparison? Orwell appears to suggest the latter explanation. This is not only a trick by a frustrated nationalist, but a case of deep self-deception, where this brand of intellectual will have abandoned the form of nationalism that lies nearest to hand without getting any closer to a genuinely internationalist outlook. He still feels the need for a Fatherland, and it is natural to look for one somewhere abroad. Having found it, he can wallow unrestrainedly in exactly those emotions from which he believes that he has emancipated himself. God, the King, the Empire, the Union Jack – all the overthrown idols can reappear under different names, and because they are not recognised for what they are, they can be worshipped with a good conscience. Transferred nationalism (.) is a way of attaining salvation without altering one's conduct.[26]

Proudly, he believes he has done away with nationalist myths. But he hasn't. Some historical artefacts are only replaced by others: Great men on horses and hagiographies about the British Empire are traded for Buddha statues and hagiographies about Gandhi. Historical kitsch is still all around – only their manifestations have changed.

We shall below argue that this masochist nationalist idealization of overseas' cultures is stronger than the extent to which positive nationalists defend their own culture. This idea may be supported by the fact that any historical kitsch defended by positive nationalists is being counter-balanced by a particular belief in social, political and economic development. Although positive nationalism depicts its domestic past in romantic colours, its sentimental self-perception is still, as it were, diffused by progress, because it sees its own culture as more developed than non-Western cultures. The historical kitsch of positive nationalism is combined with the virtues of development. Although Christianity long ago was forced upon non-Western cultures, it was nevertheless, by these early missionaries, seen as part of a progressive project.

Hence, positive nationalism can be seen as a combination of historical kitsch (regarding the sanctity of our own past) and developmental kitsch (regarding the "blessings" of our way of life and of technological progress). It should be added that indicators about child mortality, GDP, pollution, gender equality, and so on shows that this self-perception is not entirely made-up.

In dismissing historical kitsch within positive nationalism, masochist nationalists not only dismiss its conservative facets, but also the benefits of civilizational and technological superiority. Therefore, the primitive myth of masochist nationalism is not, one may claim, watered down by modernism such as reliable institutions and irrigation projects but directed squarely against progress and aimed exclusively in favour of primitivist kitsch; the blessings of nature and pre-modern communities, hostility towards modern medicine, and so on. Despite their progressive self-perception, masochist nationalists most likely surpasses positive nationalists in their attachment to primitivist images such as Rousseau's "noble savage." This lack of progressive views in the package perhaps explains why the exotic historical kitsch among masochist nationalists often is combined with a full-blown anti-modernist stance, while positive nationalism generally is associated with Enlightenment ideas. Positive nationalists are at times citizens in modern societies, and the idea of progress runs like a dim undercurrent in anything they say or do. Masochist nationalists are always citizens in progressive and successful countries (since their self-hatred is made up), but the rationale of their entire mental outlook stands in square opposition to precisely this progressive heritage.

In the West, there is an entire genre with a similar negative attitude towards modernity and a reverence for earlier times resonating with anti-Western sentiments. Stephanie Mills' Turning Away from Technology: A New Vision for the 21st Century is a good example.[27] However, as has been convincingly argued by others, such as Roger Sandall in The Culture Cult and Robert Whelan in Wild in Woods: The Myth of the Noble Eco-Savage, the belief that exotic, non-Western and primitive societies are peaceful, harmonious and "respect nature" is, if anything, associated with Western decadence and a conservative or even fascist fin-de-siècle longing for "life" – in other words to risk it. This entire historical kitsch, Jonathan West says, is nothing but "a persistent Western conceit." "Small scale, pre-agricultural, non-literate societies," West continues, "are invariably characterised by a strict sense of conformity and often extreme cruelty."[28] There is nothing wrong with expressing a desire to return to an earlier, and ostensibly more natural and peaceful way of life. The surprising thing is only that these views are held by masochist nationalists, who may swing from sentimentalism to sarcasm the moment these attitudes are fixed on their own culture. Positive nationalists, in turn, move in between the same two sentiments in the opposite direction. While they feel warmly about historical kitsch carved out of Western tradition, they are cool or even hostile against any corresponding primitivism overseas.

Ethnocentric history books

"Every nationalist," says Orwell, "is haunted by the belief that the past can be altered. He spends part of his time in a fantasy world in which things happen as they should – in which, for example, the Spanish Armada was a success, or the

24 The power of the past

Russian Revolution was crushed in 1918 – and he will transfer fragments of this world to the history books whenever possible." History books written by positive nationalists emphasize their own achievements, while those of other nations are belittled or overlooked. Their own historical figures are idealised, and their past is set in a heroic light. The purpose is chiefly to fuel nationalist emotions. Therefore, these publications contain many scientific inaccuracies. A recent case was a 2008 call by the Schusterman Centre for Jewish Studies, with the purpose to "celebrate history, literature and cultural traditions."[29] The fact that it is simply taken for granted that Jewish literature should be "celebrated" (while, presumably, Palestinian or other perspectives should not be celebrated) shows that the perspective of the Schusterman Centre for Jewish Studies is rather ethnocentric than scientific.

Masochist nationalists are quick to condemn history books written by positive nationalists. They are labelled Eurocentric, ethnocentric, monocultural, imperialist or plainly nationalist. Masochist nationalists also, however, suggest history books where a particular culture is being cherished and celebrated. But this culture is no longer here but over there. The only difference is geographic.

A good illustration of these alternative ethnocentric programs goes under the name of "Afrocentricity."[30] Afrocentricity attempts to "centralise" and "cherish" the experience and suffering of the "African person" on all levels of education. Few scholars today would seek to cherish the experience of the European, but Afrocentricity has had a considerable influence on Western academia for some time now. As early as in the 1990s, the idea was supported at a Johns Hopkins University conference, and as a case in point Shepherd Public School and Afrocentric Alternative School was opened in 2009 in Toronto, Canada, with the declared ambition to use "the sources and knowledge and experiences of peoples of African descent as an integral feature of the teaching and learning environment." Already in 1999, there were around 400 Afrocentric schools throughout the US. Recently, however, the numbers have declined due, some say, to poor academic performance and financial mismanagement.[31]

In terms of myopia and infatuation with victories and defeats, Afrocentricity is no different from any old European ethnocentricity. The "factual inaccuracies in Afrocentric writings on Egyptian history," Yehudi O. Webster comments, "are egregious and their recommended texts for history-social science instruction lack even the pretence of scholarly neutrality. The teaching of history cannot be a process of inculcating worship of ancestors."[32] Webster's criticism resembles 19th century socialists scrutinizing colonialist history writing. Exotic Afrocentricity and imperialist Eurocentricity are two words for one thing because, Banner-Haley says, Afrocentricity is "a mythology that is racist, reactionary, essentially therapeutic and is eurocentrism in black face."[33] Positive nationalists and masochist nationalists agree: History books must cherish "their" culture, and other cultures may be disregarded. At close range, they are opposites, but at a distance they are identical.

The power of the past **25**

Just as any other myopic – centricity, Afrocentricity leads to a retro-grade Balkanization and politicization of the curriculum. The current equal, non-partisan set-up of university curricula is, Diane Ravitch claims, the out-come of centuries of hard-fought campaigning. When the heirs of this struggle are throwing everything out of the window only to replace it by old-school sectarianism something drastic has occurred at the heart of the left.[34] We must support certain groups, they say. But we cannot oppose the idea of group hierar-chies by supporting another groups. The only way to counter group privileges is to oppose the principle of group selection.

We saw above how positive and masochist nationalists both seem to have little respect for the inclusive principles of a modern curriculum. They also, in a similar fashion, favour racial hierarches in education. While positive nationalists believe the "white race" to be the highest, masochist nationalists would put the "black race" on top rung. But isn't racial stereotyping part of fascist mythol-ogy? Should not, Webster wonders, "all racial myth-making studies, including Afrocentricity, be "attacked?"[35] If we oppose an idea, can we make exceptions? The questions are understandable, but they miss the point. This is not about ideas, but about geography: Everything native must be criticised and everything exotic must be hailed. As George Orwell puts it: Your own country "must be in the wrong."

Whether we talk about roots, culture, poetry, kitsch or books as cultural propaganda, both manifestations of nationalism have a similar approach to the past. To be sure, the political conviction of either is defined by a fierce antago-nism against the other. In a sense, they are saying different things. But from the point of view of a principle, they are saying the same thing.

Notes

1 Bawer, 2006, pp. 218-19.
2 SAS - "What is truly Scandinavian?"
3 'Sahlin, Mona: Sverigedemokraternas bästa vän!'
4 Kowalsky, Wolfgang, 1992, p. 64.
5 *Berlingske Tidene*, 2005.
6 "Tio minnesvärda citat av Reinfeldt," 2014.
7 "Brown sauce sales are falling: Has Britain finally come to its senses?"
8 Orwell, 1945.
9 Bosnu, Henry, "My life in media.
10 Neighboring family at the National Park Condominium, Bangkok, and overheard con-verstion: First, they spread their wings over a Somali family with a father imprisoned for overstay, and when the Somalis start sending one email after another asking for help, they say: "I mean, who do they think they are?"

- and in the reference list:
- Neighboring family at the National Park Condominium, Bangkok, and over-heard converstion, 2 April, 2016.

11 Bollywood has denigrated women.
12 West, 2005, pp. 7-8.

26 The power of the past

13 Park 51 was opened in 2011, but in the summer of 2014 it was announced that the building would serve other purposes.
14 "Im Geist des Eroberers", p. 9.
15 Orwell, 1945.
16 Caldwell, Christopher, 2010, p. 82.
17 "Därför äter vi svenskar så konstig mat."
18 Carl Snoilsky, (in Italics!) Samlade dikter (Vol. 2) (Stockholm: Hugo Gebers Förlag, 1903)
19 Stern, 1974.
20 Necef, Mehmet Ümit, ETNISK KITSCH - og andre (post)moderne fortaellingar om "de andre" (Köpenhavn: Köpenhavns Universitet, 1994)
21 Ibid., p. 152.
22 Ibid., p. 154.
23 Ibid., p. 155-6.
24 Caldwell, 2010, p. 81.
25 Orwell, 1945.
26 Ibid.
27 Mills, 1997.
28 West, 2005, p. 27.
29 Jewish Life in the Americas.
30 See, for instance, Asante, 1988.
31 The Afrocentric education crisis.
32 Webster, 1997, p. 46.
33 Banner-Haley, 2003, pp. 663-65.
34 Ravitch, 1990, p. 353.
35 Webster, 1997, p. 37.

4

THE VIRTUE OF AMNESIA AND THE VICE OF DIFFERENCE

In this chapter, three forms of similarities between positive nationalism and masochist nationalist will be dealt with. First, they cannot let go of past injustices. Second, both nationalisms are marked by group fanaticism. Third, both of them revolve around the notion of difference.

The problem of bad forgetting

Not only do positive nationalists keep presenting historical textbooks where their own past is painted in rosy colours, they also tend to brush the dust off forgotten historical events and characters, allowing them to influence daily life at the expense of the present. Within the EU, for instance, radical right-wing parties are celebrating historical events of a more than dubious repute, such as the "Committee of National Memory" created by the Greek ultra-rightist party Golden Dawn.

Nothing, in the eyes of masochist nationalists, is more appalling than dusty commemorations and old battles. Or is it? Do they really dismiss all kinds of sentimental celebrations of "peaceful" leaders who fought bravely against deceitful enemies? Do they mock anyone who wanders around with an austere face handing out leaflets filled with national-romantic propaganda? Perhaps not. After all, they are masochist nationalists: slandering themselves and getting a kick out of it while idealising all things exotic. When Muslims annually launch demonstrations in commemoration of Ashura Day, traffic comes to a standstill. In London on October 12, 2016, for instance, Oxford Street and Marble Arch were closed off, and commuters faced logistical challenges. The demonstrations carried messages like "Men and women are equal in Islam" and "Terrorism has no religion," but even the comments in Evening Standard were cautious, emphasising the demonstrations were "peaceful."[1] Why shouldn't they? In early 2010, in Malmö,

28 The virtue of amnesia; vice of difference

Sweden, a long and winding parade was held in remembrance of the martyrdom of Imam Husayn, who lived during the 7th-century. Buses were rerouted, morning programmes rescheduled, but *Sydsvenskan*, the local newspaper, never mentioned religious zealots were behind it. There were no names, no reasons nor objectives. It was all set in Heideggerian twilight as if Malmö had been hit by heavy weather. In case Germans had marched in commemoration of Bismarck, the hostile reaction in the media would have been massive.

This bending backwards to hurt feelings overseas is spilling over to the West and hurt feelings among positive nationalists. "Has not," Pascal Bruckner wonders, "a day commemorating the massacre of the rebels of the Vendée in 1793 recently been required? Why stop there?" "We think," he continues, "we are engaging in a therapeutic ritual, preventing rancour and vengeance; in fact, it is the other way around – we are awakening the rage of those who have not been mentioned, and eliciting an epidemic of claims."[2]

Enlightened Europeans, Bruce Bawer notes, have "made a point of putting their bloody past behind them."[3] Is this amnesia worth preserving? Or should we side with positive and masochist nationalists and make a career out of self-pity, envy and sheer ineptitude? "A culture without a memory cannot have a future," says a sign on Abu Dhabi Airport, an out-of-tune marriage between hostility towards the West and desire for its products. But memory is one thing and obsession is another. Obsession with the past blocks one's perception of the present and ends in political paralysis. When the past is subjective and mystical, it justifies any action whether an outsider can understand it or not. It is no longer about reality, but about being abused and humiliated, and this, we all know, cannot be questioned. The injustice is in vivid memory like a wound that never heals. Some may find this psychological profile romantic and appealing, as an emotional depth gone missing in the West. But it is in fact a handicap. Anyone with this mental set-up cannot live in the present, let alone in the future. Moreover, these people provide us with an exciting window to the past spiced up with hatred towards us. We are outsourcing history, and while they are imprisoned by it, we move on forward. It is all unspeakably heartless, even though it is presented with a fabulous political self-confidence.

Any individual caught by this mind-set – whether he or she stands on the barricades of Imperial England, Islamic resurrection or any other revival – is incapable of forgiveness, because forgiveness requires forgetting, and forgetting is forbidden. This particular sickness is not a case of bad remembrance, but of bad forgetting. Recent studies, Richards and Frankland claims, "provide evidence that forgetting is necessary for flexible behaviour in dynamic environments."[4] In a social system in constant flux, Brea and others maintain, "it was important for an agent to engage in gradual forgetting; otherwise, behaviour remained inflexible and the overall reward rate declined."[5] A comparison with different political mind-sets is perhaps not far-fetched, where sentimental nationalists indulging in long-gone cases of injustice in the middle of the "dynamic environment" of capitalism will appear inflexible and face an "overall reward rate decline(.)".

Masochist nationalists show no remorse for positive nationalists obsessed by historical cases of injustice against their own culture. Still, with no sense of inner confusion masochist nationalists rush to the support of historical celebrations by overseas cultures and the more outlandish and awe-inspiring, the more it tickles our collective sense of self-abasement. Judging from their contradictory views on collective memory, masochist nationalists have no consistent opinion about nationalism. Hence, this aspect can be subtracted from the equation. Left on the paper is a dismissive attitude towards their home country's collective struggle. This self-flagellation is not based on factual events because the past of the West is not more guilt-ridden than the past of other regions of the world.[6] Instead, it is based on Western masochism – pleasure in pain and excitement in remorse.

Group fanaticism

Turning from a shared fixation with history to an obsessive admiration towards one's own group, this quality offers another common trait, even though masochist nationalists pretend to offer a complete break not only with group fanaticism at home, but everywhere and as a principle.

Positive nationalists can be called group fanatics. The group – constituted by the domestic nation – is hailed as of supreme importance. Sometimes, it even acquires organic features, while its individuals are rendered faceless and disposable. Adam Müller, 19th-century reactionary state theorist, saw the individual as a mere atom in the state organism, and today Nikolaos Michaloliakos, leader of the Greek ultra-rightist Golden Dawn, says "individuals do not have historical significance."[7] The organic metaphors within positive nationalism imply a head that does all the thinking (the leader), and a body that does all the acting (the people). The "benevolent" leader acts "unselfishly" on behalf of his grateful crowd excited by this larger-than-life experience. This romantic cliché implies an identity of interest between leader and his people. The class tension between high and low is gone. Representatives are no longer elected based on political ideas, but as a result of "shared historical experience." Insiders and outsiders are carefully separated. Horizontal intimacy is combined with vertical estrangement.

Masochist nationalist rarely miss an opportunity to expose this group fanaticism to the public. But when focus is shifted to their own spiritual home overseas, this critical stance is subject to nothing short of a political metamorphosis. While the positive nationalist goes out of his way to defend the organic unity of one particular group – the domestic nation – the masochist nationalist goes out of his way to defend organic myths in another group – the culture overseas. Positive nationalism often deteriorates into an odd, monstrous individualism where the nation as a whole turns into an ogre, only to be matched by the preferred image of the masochist nationalist – an exotic culture with feet of clay.

30 The virtue of amnesia; vice of difference

The brutality of Robert Mugabe was only slowly recognised among masochist nationalists in the West. Zimbabwe was finally free from oppression, and now, under his guidance, black people had the opportunity to build up the country in peaceful cooperation. White man bad – black man good. When Mugabe threw lavishing birthday parties in the middle of a crisis it was seen as an expression of the pride of black people of Zimbabwe. The poor was laughing along with the rich.

A corresponding idea where "white people" are freed from "black people" would be hard to find outside the far-right fringes. The fact that masochist nationalists may confuse Ahmadinejad and Iranian communists based on their "shared background" illustrate the group fanaticism outlined above. In Nomad, Ayaan Hirsi Ali tells the story of UN distributions of food. Rations are handed over to people who claim to be clan leaders. But instead of portioning it out, they keep it for themselves or sell it.[8] Why is it assumed that the relation between individuals in these societies is harmonious? If it was, why do they need UN assistance? When our pet ideas of anti-racism and exoticism are at stake, reality is the first victim. Save for the detail of replacing domestic for exotic, masochist nationalists are no different from their positive counterparts in dismissing the struggle between classes.

If attention is turned from exotic nations to overseas' individuals in the West, they all vanish into a "culture." We have already mentioned the IT specialist from the Ivory Coast, who was asked to "express his culture" and cook native food although he never did it. This is the background to the ways in which encounters between two individuals from different cultures are being described. It is not simply two people having a talk but something perversely majestic – a "meeting between cultures" likely to provoke wild enthusiasm and conference papers. This whirlwind of group mysticism is not found in some dusty books from the age of colonialism, but in endless documents crafted by today's masochist nationalists – colonialism's most ruthless critics.

The masochist nationalist myth of organic harmony of distant cultures, whether far-off or as migrants in the West, leads to another issue. In the West, parliaments are supposed to favour "minority representation." The idea is that the pluralist community is already in shambles; white positive nationalists favour each other so why shouldn't others do the same? This rests on the assumption that minorities in the West are homogeneous, untroubled by political and religious tensions. Any spokesperson speaks on behalf of the entire group. An Iranian gives voice to his Iranian co-patriots. Positive nationalist old belief in unity between representative and Volk is now given a brush or two and proudly presented as an emancipating idea for the benefit of minority populations. Empowering over there, suffocating at home.

In Europe, only a positive nationalist would suggest any one of us could "represent" others in an overseas' parliament by means of shared background only. No matter how much a member of the Bulgarian proto-fascist Ataka would insist on common heritage, left-wing Bulgarians would still not accept

The virtue of amnesia; vice of difference **31**

to be represented by this person in a foreign political assembly. "Common origin" and "ancestry," we learned in school, are euphemisms for reactionary rule. We need to hold on to ideas and principles. But regarding ethnic minorities in the West subject to fatal political tension, we ignore political views altogether and lump individuals – oppressors and dissidents alike – together in one box labelled "Syrian Nationals" or "Iraqi co-patriots." Western societies are fairly homogeneous, characterised by social trust as a result of some degree of political freedom, while the oppression in Iran, ironically, has left the country deeply fractured. But masochist nationalists are undeterred by this. Western nations must cherish diversity, and are not allowed to aspire for solidarity, commonalities and unity – because this, we are told, would amount to "exclusion" and "racism." Troubled cultures overseas, on the other hand, simply have to be blessed by political communion because they must unite against Western oppression. Warm-hearted Germans, for instance, prefer to talk about Iranians' "shared historical experience" instead of addressing "condescending" views about political disputes in the country, and when Iranian journalists and left-wingers raise concern it is not always taken seriously and journalists may wonder whether a negative image of Iran might not, in fact, boost support for right-wing populist parties – in Germany. Voting points here appears more important than bloodshed overseas. One would assume positive nationalists to be behind this self-preoccupation, but in fact masochist nationalists and "anti-racists" are behind it. Whether you dismiss cultures overseas or find them enchanting and superior, the end result is cultural self-obsession and nationalism – whether "positive" or "negative".

Germany has been underestimating violence against dissidents by terrorist proxies linked to the Teheran regime, such as the 1992 Mykonos Restaurant assassinations in Berlin. "The calm professionalism of the Mykonos killers is emblematic of the ruthlessness with which the Islamic Republic has consistently sought to counter its political opponents," Iran Human Rights Documentation Centre commented.[9] Regime critics seek refuge due to political oppression. But the one aspect not considered by the host country is political tension. The class issue is all but dead. Instead, we speak soothingly about "ethnic origin" while flogging our own backs in public display. Out of kindness we give them nightmares. Left-wing dissidents are under attack by religious reactionaries, but Westerners offer no help. One should note that these Westerners are not positive nationalists caring little for left-wingers, but masochist nationalists claiming to fight against conservative oppression.

In the discussion on positive nationalism above, only the most radical would suggest selecting political representatives by means of mythic bonds with fellow citizens. In a modern society, political qualifications count, as opposed to "origin" and "roots." But precisely these problems keep haunting those who cherish overseas' cultures or minorities in the West. Anne Phillips talks about "politics of presence," where a minority candidate is selected by means of ethnic ancestry instead of political ideas. This multicultural idea, she claims, easily deteriorates

32 The virtue of amnesia; vice of difference

into mysticism, where lack of political experience can be met with aloof proclamations about shared group identity.[10] While ethnic representatives acquire godly features, community members turn blank-faced and disposable. This is not a new idea. Idealization of group representatives along with an assault against the common person was always part of positive nationalist visions, whether in Nazi Germany, Mussolini's Italy, or any other.

Masochist nationalists attack European politicians who dismiss ideological cleavages and defend common national ancestry. The Greek Golden Dawn and the Bulgarian Ataka are cases in point.[11] Outside of the West, however, hardcore nationalism is reframed as "self-determination." From a distance, masochist nationalists are not critical against group fanaticism. They are merely against group thinking at home while approaching groups elsewhere with wide-eyed reverence. This is nationalism in its transposed form; militant calls for multiculturalism and "diversity" at home as mirror image of overseas' group fanaticism. Why not instead endorse a balanced and reasoned nationalism here and elsewhere – closely linked to democratic institutions such as the welfare state and the rule of law? What is the motive behind those who pour venom on group identity in the West, only to resurface as group mystics in far-off land?

A final example of this joint group fanaticism relates to the concept of "identity." Not long ago, it was linked to the individual, as in "personal identity," indicating independence and free choice.[12] In this interpretation, identity had very little in common with reverence for a group. Rather, it signalled the opposite. But lately this meaning has been cornered by a different interpretation – namely "identity" as compliance with an ethnic group, implying dependence and lack of free choice. The concept of "identity" is used by those who espouse the individual's submission to the group but wish to phrase is more conveniently.

Two cases come to mind on the side of positive nationalists. The "Identitarians" suggest a conceited and yet submissive "identity" between individual and culture, asserting the right of "Europeans" to Europe's culture and territory. Alternative für Deutschland – AfD – a German right-wing party – refers to "German Identity," bringing up, some say, reminiscences from the country's past by suggesting a unified Volk lining up against "intruders" and "disruptive" outsiders. This right-wing group fanaticism is, however, reflected on the opposite side of the political spectrum. This goes under the name of "Identity politics" or "Multiculturalism" – masochist nationalists' official academic doctrine. In order to show the extent of its fusion of individual and culture from a (supposedly) left-wing perspective, we should return to the group cult of the Greek ultra-rightist party Golden Dawn above. The group fanaticism among multiculturalists, namely, seems to be a reverse replica of nothing short of the political program of a Greek right-wing party where the label "fascist" – for once – seems accurate. In the eyes of radical-right wingers, the charismatic leader – or Führer – is "the head" that does all the thinking while the body (the people) acts out his message. In the theory of identity politics, a vital function is carried out by the "ethnic representative" or "community leader," who acts on behalf of his (rarely "her") downtrodden ethnic members. Both camps make use of the same political images. The crowds surrounding the extreme right-wing leader are grateful and silent, and the description of any text-book classic multicultural gathering shows the same features of submissive ecstasy. On either side, class tensions are replaced by a most intimate – although not necessarily convincing – relation between the spokesperson and his crowd. Both a far right-wing leader and a left-wing community representative have very little political experience, but all the more sense of "community," and ability to "identify" historically in terms of mutual struggle and suffering with his passionate herd underneath. The abuse of the individual – the litmus test of any collectivist fantasy – is equally pronounced in both camps. While Golden Dawn, as we saw above, denies the individual a "historical significance," you can sit through hours of multicultural debate without the individual being mentioned once, even as a target of criticism. In fact, a multiculturalist pays even less attention to the individual than a state romantic, to whom the concrete individual occupies the centre of the entire analysis. Above all, finally, both positive and masochist nationalism rest on the expectation of an airtight identity between leader and follower – in other words on group fanaticism. It is worth restating that the proto-fascist Golden Dawn appears to offer a corresponding image in terms of group cult to a movement – Identity politics – widely cherished for its "anti-racist" foundation.

Conclusively, another similarity should be addressed. Both nationalists are trying to fuel support for right-wing parties; positive nationalists for obvious reasons, and masochist nationalists as a result of their tactically counter-productive left-wing sectarianism.

Ever since the end of World War II, Wolfgang Kowalsky notes, those on the left have tainted any reference to "German identity." This unwillingness to acknowledge that Germany today – rather than Nazism – is associated with an economic powerhouse and an extensive humanitarian policy has meant that the entire identity rhetoric, perfectly sound and edifying in moderation, has been abandoned by political mainstream. Any German who would say identity is a good thing runs the risk of being dismissed as far-right winger. As a result of this unforgiving attitude among influential parts of the elites, values of belonging, safety, intimacy, love and even family are being branded as politically poisonous. The tragedy, then, is that the public reactions do not follow the elite's expectations. Citizens do not generally conclude that social-conservative values are in fact extreme right-wing. This mental artistry is confined to our rootless masochist nationalist, with a lifestyle as jet-setting single. Instead, the proximity is solved by concluding that if family values are tainted by fascism, fascism cannot be all that bad. Right-wing views, in other words, will not be shunned by the general public, but swiftly dragged into political mainstream where they will constitute an ever-increasing temptation. If you belong to the politically disinterested Somewheres instead of the Anywheres – as this division is framed

34 The virtue of amnesia; vice of difference

by David Goodhart, your family is more important to you than any ideology. They are therefore radicalised politically instead of being transformed to bloodless Anywheres.[13]

This refusal to acknowledge the benefits of the idea of identity at home not only boosts the support of far right-wing parties, but also brutalises the political discussion. "The danger," Kowalsky continues, "associated with this leftist taboo is barely acknowledged."[14] Masochist nationalists are flirting with group fanaticism and collectivist myths overseas while radicalising the electorate in Europe.

Is there anything in this, then, that would upset positive nationalists? Very little, it seems. A general audience infuriated by their opponent's accusations of having fascist views is clearly in their own interest, and so is a brutalised public discussion along with escalating political radicalization. Positive nationalists can spend their time on other things, if political mainstream is caving in as a result of masochist nationalist suicidal agitation. When masochist nationalists are busy marginalising themselves into oblivion, positive nationalists can only watch the tragedy unfolding. As for the general idea of group fanaticism, the positive nationalist would stand firmly behind the masochist nationalist – even though their respective culture of emotional identification is very different.

Obsession with difference

The fact that masochist nationalists fail to counter group fanaticism as such, but merely criticise its domestic appearance, also means they are tempted by another of nationalism's pitfalls – an obsession with difference. The idea of a uniform culture is linked to the idea of difference; i.e. clear borders to other cultures.

Unlike liberal criticism against positive nationalism, where boastful claims of being collectively different are being questioned by means of progressive belief in solidarity and human rights, masochist nationalists have come full circle. They are equally infatuated by difference. While one is grabbing you by the throat, saying: "We are different!" – another is nailing you with his eyes, whispering: "They are different!" Even though the man from the Ivory Coast above was a software engineer engaged in global, culturally unspecific matters, he was pushed back to his "cultural background." Please be different! Computers are ok, but obscure ethnic traditions are so much more interesting. Our superiority, based on emotions, has been replaced by their pre-eminence, resting on little more than self-humiliation and ignorance about cultures overseas.

Far right-wingers claim a common cultural background is a prerequisite for appreciation. Any difference, such as another language, shuts the door for it. Masochist nationalists, then, say something opposite and yet similar. While they fail to show appreciation for their own culture, they can barely hide their enthusiasm for anything different, obscure and impenetrable. Sitting on the Bangkok

The virtue of amnesia; vice of difference **35**

BTS surrounded by Thai, a language they do not understand, they experience – or at least make every effort in this direction – how their imagination is suddenly brimming with those feelings they are barred from expressing at home out of political reasons – enthusiasm, sympathy, curiosity and wonder.

But why would difference and lack of understanding cause enthusiasm and feelings of sympathy? Are not these feelings, rather, connected with the presence of understanding, of shared views and being equal? As noted by Kenan Malik, the "principle of difference cannot provide any standards that oblige us to respect the 'difference' of others. At best, it invites our indifference to the fate of the Other." On a sunny day, we just don't care. "At worst," Malik continues, "it licenses us to hate and abuse those who are different. Why, after all, should we not abuse and hate them?"[15] We hear the distant echo of positive nationalism. Why endorse masochist nationalist difference, when difference positive nationalist style is not to be trusted? Why is that wall of separation appealing only from the other side? Regarding positive nationalism, we all know its claims to difference open the gates for violence. Why, then, should masochist nationalist difference – resting on an identical set of shady sentiments – be any different? Masochist nationalism expresses the same self-righteousness as positive nationalism, and claims to be different, special and unusual. Whether this idealised land is here or elsewhere is less important. When the National Socialists started their atrocities against the Jews, they were not portrayed as similar to the Germans, but as different and alien, as an odd and distant breed. One might speculate if the Holocaust ever had come under sway, had the Berlin propaganda machinery instead announced Jews were not different, but similar to the Germans, and equal in all respects. If we take off those distorting spectacles of "difference," it all becomes clear: respect requires equality, and lack of respect rests on difference. The Holocaust, Hannah Arendt says, was only possible by first depriving the Jews of their humanity, i.e. making them different. The Jews did not celebrate their enforced difference but cursed it. The Nazis singled out the Jews for extermination. Masochist nationalists single out people from overseas hoping to avoid it. The outcome is likely to be equally terrifying, whether you adhere to the principle of difference out of hatred or out of misconceived compassion.

The reason why masochist nationalists have put all their stakes on difference is also because they have been taught by postmodernism, post-colonialism and other popular academic disciplines that similarity – including solidarity, equal rights, and feelings of community – essentially was right-wing extreme. An interesting case is a recent web-ad at Malmö University College where Adolf Hitler was defined as an enemy of multiculturalism because multiculturalism is "anti-racist."[16] In case you oppose the Holocaust, then, you must embrace multiculturalism and difference which, as we saw above, was a prerequisite of the Holocaust.

Masochist nationalism resembles positive nationalism. Masochist nationalists are also fuelled by the belief in hierarchies, in a mythical perception of history,

36 The virtue of amnesia; vice of difference

and also, guided by the fatal attraction of "difference and diversity," in a heartless attitude towards minorities under siege, Jews and others.

This shared obsession with difference is dangerous from another point of view. If similarities and equality are ideologically tainted, and we rush towards difference, how are we to prevent difference from spilling over to economic matters? Why not also cherish difference in wealth? Why should not the rich fight for the right of the poor to remain poor? As the political theorist Nancy Fraser noted, "The remedy required to redress injustice [has become] cultural recognition, as opposed to political-economic redistribution."[17] While a socialist in the past facing poverty brought it to attention because no human beings should live without dignity, today's masochist nationalists witness the same distressing circumstances without doing anything at all, because difference is "a good thing," and any attempt to change it is a violation against a "fragile culture." These implications of difference and cultural recognition are deeply conservative. There is no social change or emancipation in masochist nationalism, apart from the emancipation of their own conscience when they realise any attempt to transform the conditions of the down-beaten is tantamount to racism. We used to be concerned about our wealth. Now we celebrate their poverty. This book is no attempt to defend the positive nationalist. In this particular instance it is perhaps, though, a deeper sin to ignore the browbeaten under the pretence of warm-hearted diversity and anti-racism along with an absolute conviction of being in the right, than to avoid and belittle their suffering and, yet, realise that somehow this is not right and that everything one day has to change.

Also, from an economic point of view, masochist nationalism may easily drift towards sentiments inseparable from positive nationalism. If the key to fight injustice is cultural difference and recognition instead of social development, an aloof elite has found a great way to justify their arrogance. If they are searching for a mask to cover up their hostility towards social change, few ideas would beat masochist nationalists' sentimental attitude to social deprivation – as long as it is not culturally recognizable but "different." If they fear widespread, muscular economic emancipation of overseas cultures, what could be better than conflating liberation with violation, oppression, and racism? What we are witnessing here is an important link between positive and masochist nationalists, namely the fact that the former for the sake of class exploitation may profit from the latter's exoticism. The entire picture, as we shall return to below, is a combination of politically perplexed left-wingers and clear-sighted right-wingers.

Notes

1 "Ashura Day 2016".
2 Bruckner, 2010, p. 109.
3 Bawer, 2006, p. 157.
4 Richards and Frankland, 2017, pp. 1071-84.
5 Brea, et al., 2014.

6 In case facets of European history are not as dark as one may wish, one can always modify it, to make it fit into this self-abusive scheme. At Swedish universities, for instance, students are taught "post-colonial theory", even though Sweden was never a colonial power.
7 Adamson, 2016b, p. 42.
8 Hirsi Ali, 2008, p. 157.
9 Iran Human Rights Documentation Centre.
10 Phillips, 1995.
11 For an ideological comparison of four members of the European far-right family, see Adamson, 2016b, pp. 38–46.
12 See, for instance, Parfit, 1984.
13 Goodhart, 2017.
14 Kowalsky, 1992, p. 16.
15 Malik, Can multiculturalism work?, 2002.
16 Adolf Hitler – Mångfaldens fiende.
17 Fraser, 1995, p. 75.

5

THE PURPOSE OF ART, WELL, THAT'S REALLY NONE OF OUR BUSINESS

We shall now turn to artistic freedom. Positive and masochist nationalists, it will be maintained, are mirroring each other's moves. The question whether the artist or the art critic should be protected or put in jail depends, as it seems, on whether he or she is politically agreeable. It is all about ideological self-interest, and very little about the principle of artistic freedom.

A "cheap provocation, openly racist and hostile against Hungary."[1] The words belong to Vince Szalay Bobrovniczky, Hungarian Ambassador to Austria, after an art exhibition in Linz in 2013, where Hungarian treatment of Roma was compared to the way Jews were treated under National Socialism. Bobrovniczky raised the issue with the Mayor of Linz, and then sent a letter to Federal President Heinz Fischer, demanding that the exhibition be closed. In 2012, the same posters had been showcased at a construction site in Linz and were destroyed after complaints by Hungarian nationalists. Following a parliamentary question to the Minister of Interior, the Linz Police formally apologised to the artist, and Joseph Weidenholzer, a Social Democratic MP, rushed to the artist's support: "In terms of freedom of political art, which has to be provocative, we want to show the exhibition again."[2] The looming shadow of National Socialism fell over Bobrovniczky. His comments about a "provocation" being "hostile against Hungary" echoed, it was argued, Hitler's inauguration speech at the 1937 Entartete Kunst exhibition, that, said Hitler, "insults German feelings."[3]

The following year, in Sweden, a similar conflict ensued. In Halmstad and Nyköping, public schools featured mural paintings of vaginas by the artist Carolina Falkholt. "Artists who paint private parts should be in jail," Margareta Larsson, then MP of the Sweden Democrats, announced in parliament. "Meter-sized vaginas" on school walls, she said, "is inappropriate." Instead, art should "have a purpose." Lars Ohly, former Communist leader, shot back: "This perception of art and culture is straight from Germany in the 30s". Once again,

The purpose of art **39**

the critic was tarnished with National Socialism. "The fact that these views are presented by a member of Swedish parliament," Ohly continued, "is abhorrent and highly remarkable." "The purpose of art, well, that's really none of our business."[4]

A reassuring line of demarcation arises, or so it seems. On the one hand Bobrovniczky and Larsson – opponents of artistic freedom from their towers of privilege – and on the other hand Weidenholzer and Ohly, advocates of l'art pour l'art, witnessing their opponents' exercise in power with justified discomfort. When state interest trumps artistic freedom, Germany in the 1930s comes to mind. If political art is not provocative, it is not political. Art is none of our business.

The problem is only that art in your own taste might say little about your approach towards artistic freedom as a principle. What if Weidenholzer and Ohly were merely defending art out of ideological reasons, as if artistic freedom is an issue on par with, for instance, taxation? They were both, after all, on the left, and the objects of their criticism were right-wingers. The true test is when we are confronted with art we oppose, and whose advocates' political views are very different from our own. Would Weidenholzer and Ohly stand the test of artistic freedom? Are their strong sentiments based on a principle, or do they merely come out as masochist nationalists opposing anything Western while endorsing all things exotic – i.e. as positive nationalists with the coat inside out?

In August 2007, Lars Vilks, Swedish artist and Professor in art theory, gained international fame by publishing a drawing of a roundabout dog with the face of Muhammed in Nerikes Allehanda – a Swedish local newspaper. An Al-Qaeda group placed a $100,000 bounty on his head. His house was torched. Several times his life has been in danger, such as the 2015 gunfire against Krudttönden in central Copenhagen. Protected day and night by the Swedish Police, he is constantly changing lodgings while trying to maintain an intimate relationship. There is a parallel case. In 2014, Swedish street artist Dan Park opened an exhibition featuring collage posters, one of them displaying a black student activist naked, in chains. A message said: "Our negro slave has run away" along with the student's contact information. In Copenhagen 2016, Vilks gave a lecture about different interpretations of Park's posters, none of them necessarily more true than any other. When art is being discussed in court, Vilks explained, an expert is present to show the difference between art and information and to prevent simplified conclusions about what the artist actually "means." "There is no real discussion in Sweden," Park claims, "and I am trying to provoke a discussion about political correctness."[5]

On the surface there were now different issues at stake, and artist and critic had traded places. Conservatives were no longer under fire by left-wingers. Instead, groups under the patronage of the left – radical Muslims and Blacks – were targeted by people deemed as rightists. Still, from the point of view of principle, little had changed. Provocative artists were under attack by intolerant adversaries. So how did those left-wingers respond to Vilks and Park – the same

40 The purpose of art

left-wingers who above had defended artistic freedom when the artist was on their side?

When a few paintings above had mocked Hungary, its right-wing ambassador had labelled it an insult to his country, and he had been ridiculed by left-wingers. Now, the same left-wingers said Vilks' roundabout dog was "an insult against Muslims." An ageing news-anchor grabbed the opportunity by saying Vilks was merely referring to "freedom of speech (.) in order to humiliate Muslims" – and one of the key figures in the Church of Sweden piously maintained, in a phrase that mirrored the Hungarian Ambassador, that "time has come to distance ourselves from Vilks' blasphemies."[6] The Church of Sweden, worth noting, is a good example of the left's "March through the institutions." It is a hothouse of anti-Western masochist nationalists.[7]

Some of those above who had defended artistic freedom had now made a political U-turn with no sense of inner contradiction. The communist Lars Ohly, for instance, who'd said art's purpose is "none of our business," could now suddenly be heard from the other camp. "It was important to bear in mind," he announced, "that Vilks' ambition with his art is to fuel racism and Islamophobia."[8] Ohly had failed the test of artistic freedom. He only embraced it when the artist was on his side politically. Above, Ohly and Weidenholzer had accused art critics for evoking National Socialism. Now, left-wing allegations of National Socialism was instead targeting the artist.

But what about Dan Park? Wouldn't his art, at least, be rescued by left-wingers who had come to understand they were dealing with a precious political principle instead of one or other passing manifestation of it? Judging by this investigation, none of those who would be on the barricades against the "Nazi" Hungarian Ambassador or the Swedish MP, had any consolation for Dan Park. As his case travelled through the press in 2014, his art was unanimously dismissed as abusive and degrading against black people, as if everyone knew exactly what he meant by it.[9]

And what about the infatuation above, of spending your time watching things you strongly oppose while being disturbed by it? From a liberal point of view, there are plenty of things for all of us do engage in, and we shouldn't waste our time on things we don't like. If you don't like chess, you don't watch it, and it would not be right to tell others to stop playing. The positive nationalists above, however, were more ambitious. The Hungarian Ambassador and the Swedish MP kept looking at the pictures they found offensive and eventually demanded they should be taken down, because they didn't like them.

The reaction to art from the other camp was, however, no different. Faced with Lars Vilks' roundabout dog with a face of Muhammed, his critics could have proven him wrong by looking elsewhere. But they didn't and so proved him right. Caught in a discussion about his art, Lars Vilks once replied: "If you don't like it, don't look at it."[10] If we try to shut down exhibitions we oppose, logic will break down, because I may oppose your desire to put an end to other's pleasures. Positive nationalists try to stop left-wing art mocking the West.

The purpose of art **41**

Masochist nationalists seek to prohibit art defending the West. They are both reactionaries, out-of-place creatures in the 21st-century.

How, then, did this ungenerous attitude manifest itself? The Linz exhibition, we saw above, was simply destroyed following "complaints" by Hungarian Nationalists in the face of shocked left-wingers, who now, witnessing Park's art, were as shocked, to the extent they took him to court and ordered the destruction of nine of his posters, in the face of alarmed right-wingers. With surprising ease, left and right-wingers were trading opinions and emotions. They were both abusing the idea of artistic freedom for the benefit of their respective political conviction.

Another similarity between positive and masochist nationalists relates to the common view that art must have "a purpose." It is not enough to be provocative. Art must also be edifying. Historically, this rhetoric belonged to the conservative first line of defence against left-wing artists' "insults" and attacks against "decency" and "good taste." While radicals say art should reflect an ugly world, conservatives say it should give us guidance and beauty. When the Swedish right-wing MP is infuriated by nudity in public, art demanding it must have a purpose, she is merely giving voice to this age-old attitude. But now from the left came similar accusations too many to mention, as if they hadn't been penned by a leftist at all. "Lars Vilks' roundabout dog," a south Swedish newspaper commented, was a "mockery with no purpose," and Ilmar Reepalu, for decades the head of Social Democracy in Malmö, who had overlooked the exodus of Jews from the city with surprising indifference, claimed Vilks' exhibition was only being put on for "political ends," hoping "no one will visit the gallery."[11] Denouncing Vilks' exhibition as "only" political, Reepalu was rejecting politics as a sufficient purpose in art. Surprisingly, a left-winger, resting on a proud tradition where artistic provocation was a means of survival, was now dragging down political art to the level of empty provocation. In case Reepalu would have the ambition to oppose that disquieting conservative idea where art is merely state propaganda, because any "purpose" is always in the interest of some and to the detriment of others, he would have to dismiss also the political exhibition in Linz above, where Hungarian treatment of Roma was compared to Nazi treatment of Jews. But probably he wouldn't. He would only mimic conservative arrogance from the other end. As a masochist nationalist, he would scorn Vilks, a white, male Westerner – overlooking the fact that Vilks – a classic leftist, had dared to provoke massive retaliation from religious reactionaries, whom Reepalu, then, would idealise as "victims of Western colonialism."

We should also remember Weidenholzer, the Social Democratic MP above, who had defended the artist where Hungary was being compared to Nazi Germany. Political art, Weidenholzer had announced "has to be provocative." Politics provided art with a purpose, and a provocation was the icing on the cake. Reepalu, on his part, had complained that Vilks' art was "only political," suggesting politics was an insufficient purpose in art. But these contradictions go away if we admit that the principle of artistic freedom means as much for those

42 The purpose of art

modern-day leftists as it ever meant for old conservatives. This is not about an idea but about ideology. The two social democrats are merely engaged in different conflicts. In Reepalu's shoes, Weidenholzer would probably also dismiss Vilks' art as "only political," and, in the shoes of the Austrian, Reepalu would most likely announce there are few nobler forms of art than political art – and yes – it has to be provocative. Moving from art mocking the West to art supporting it, left-wingers would be trading opinions, convictions, and moral indignation with no visible trace of inner struggle.

This dismissive attitude towards political art, moreover, is hard to combine with any left-of-centre conviction. Suggesting art cannot be grounded in politics and must be supplanted by an aesthetic or edifying justification was always a sign of conservative political oppression. Your political statement demanding autonomy and pluralism is not allowed, but my political statement aimed at constricting you is allowed. The Social democrats' attack against Vilks, then, can only be understood as a display of conservative power against progressive artistic rebellion.

Which brings us over to a more fundamental problem about the particular left-wing art critics in this discussion. The whole idea that art must have a purpose is, as I mentioned above, part of conservative rhetoric. Whatever left-wing art criticism can do, it's history and theory does not allow to make use of opponents' argument. If they still do, if they, for instance, claim Vilks' art must have a purpose, disregarding his successful political art as "empty" or "meaningless," they are engaged in a conservative and bourgeois art criticism clamping down on threats to decency and established order. Bringing up morality or the virtues of a left-wing ideological perspective is just another authoritarian way of dismissing artistic freedom. If the left abandons its traditional role of defending l'art pour l'art and, say, Duchamp's "Fountain" as a rebellious act, the whole idea of modern art breaks apart.

One should, however, bear in mind that the entire scheme of leftist rebellion in the arts versus conservative outrage belongs to a time when the establishment was conservative and the artists young and radical. Now, when the left has made impressive inroads into the establishment, its attitude towards art is also becoming increasingly conservative and authoritarian. When left-wingers now attack "indecent" art, they have become part of the elite, and why shouldn't they, in all but name, adjust their approach and suggested treatment of dissenting artists to that of the establishment? Why would Weidenholzer and Ohly, for instance, remain faithful to the principles of left-wing artistic rebellion, when their allegiances within their new-found elite surroundings might be so much more tempting? If class-based identification is part of left-wing analysis, shouldn't it also, then, apply for left-wing class-travellers? In order to retain their vested interests and privileges, these new-found establishment leftists have moreover taken the opportunity to redefine artistic rebellion as right-wing extreme. They have managed to create a situation where their own elitism goes under the name of anti-racism, and they have been amply celebrated by their own media apparatus for it. Not long ago, a conservative establishment took the opportunity to brand any artistic rebellion as a call for revolution, and it was supported by its own newspapers for doing it. These are important connections between positive and masochist nationalism.

There are superficial differences and deeper affinities. "The Communist and the Catholic," says George Orwell, "are not saying the same thing, in a sense they are even saying opposite things, and each would gladly boil the other in oil if circumstances permitted; but from the point of view of an outsider they are very much alike."[12] A left-wing establishment, it goes without saying, is different from a right-wing establishment. The particular groups protected by one may be imprisoned by the other. And yet, the underlying pattern is very similar. A mere glance at the mechanisms of hegemonic power and the ways in which dissidents are being dealt with show, it seems, that the entire elitist machinery can be handed by a left-winger or a right-winger without shifting a single bolt. Left-wing social climbers do not replace a right-wing establishment with an opposite set of values. Both left-wingers and right-wingers acquire the common class sentiments and social attitudes of the establishment.

From here on and the issue of art's purpose, there is an adjacent discussion about whether the artist is "good" or "poor." No comments were found along those lines among the right-wingers above – saying it was all technically "poor quality" or "I could have done that," but these kinds of allegations belong to the standard repertoire when conservatives defend figurative art and artistic crafts-manship against left-wing provocations, such as the art movement Dadaism or Kasimir Malevitj's "*White square on a white background*" – suggesting we have to start everything anew. More interesting, however, is the fact that the left have adopted the same conservative rhetoric. Left-wingers, too, attack "poor quality" in art whenever it suits their ideological preferences. "The quality of (Vilks') work is to say the least far below even mediocre," an art critic claimed, and "the art is of poor quality and only meant to insult."[13] Save for the fact that the politi-cal coat has come inside out, it is hard to tell apart from upper-class arrogance of the past. Jan Guillou, influential left-winger, took the opportunity to disqualify Vilks' technical qualities as an artist: "He can't draw," and the newspaper *Svenska Dagbladet* took it even further, saying Vilks decided "to make a thing out of his bad artistic craftsmanship."[14] Regarding Dan Park, a curator and critic spoke for the entire art scene: "Park's art," he announced, "is an artistic failure," and "from all essential aspects, he lacks relevance in the eyes of the players in the art field." Park, he concluded, "is not even a bad or an underdeveloped artist."[15] But who says Park's art is a failure? Who defines art's "essential aspects?" Wasn't this, during early 20th-century, part of an increasingly defensive conservative cul-tural agitation? And wasn't that kind of rhetoric the source of amusement among radical artists in London and Paris? Street artists always try to provoke, and the curator, an insider, was now dancing to the choreography of Dan Park – a brow-beaten outsider. Was Igor Stravinsky's *Rite of Spring* an attempt to appease "the players in the art field?" Resting, as he most certainly did, on a radical tradition

44 The purpose of art

of artistic rebellion, the curator had every opportunity to see beyond the quagmire of personal preferences and defend Park's no matter what. But instead, he chose to attack Park in a way that, in anything but name, smacked with bourgeois establishment arrogance. Yesterday, establishment conservatives used their heavy fist against "poor quality," and today, establishment left-wingers attack artists who "can't draw." For conservatives, this is to be expected. For left-wingers, it is a betrayal of their tradition of artistic rebellion.

There are also more hands-on signs that the old antagonism between left and right has faded. A right-wing MP, we mentioned above, claimed artists "who paint private parts should be in jail." Indeed, another case of conservative upper-class extravaganza. If you make art we disapprove of, we will put you behind bars. The left-wing clarion call of l'art pour l'art was lying on the floor, glass shattered. Luckily, her demand fell on deaf ears, she was roundly ridiculed, and soon thereafter she became an independent. The left, then, could have realised that the only way to counter these echoes from the past is to stick to the principle of artistic freedom. Artists do not belong in jail. But again, the left cared little for principles, but all the more for their own political agenda. They were shocked at the sight of right-wingers trying to jail left-wing artists, and they were as shocked now at the sight of Park – penned "a right-wing artist" – to the extent they sentenced Park to jail. As opposed to the right-wing MP, whose suggestion was rightly scorned, the same suggestion from the left quickly gained wide acclaim among journalists, politicians and lawyers throughout Sweden. Dan Park was sentenced to six months "for incitement to racial agitation and defamation." Evidently, and as I will get back to shortly, the court knew exactly how to interpret Park's art. Or rather, it wasn't a case of interpretation at all. His art was racist, and anyone could see that.

But there was more to it. In case the right-wingers had suggested fining the artists defended by Weidenholzer and Ohly, they would barely have believed it. The opposite scenario, however, not only happened but passed almost unnoticed, and left-wing sympathies shifted from victim to establishment. Dan Park was fined 60,000 Swedish kronor in damages, and no one was struck by its fatal contradiction.[16] It was left-wing hypocrisy at its most naked. Fining a left-wing artist is like the 1930s, but you can penalise any artist if only you put a sticker of right-winger on his forehead. We should have no illusions about far right-wingers' approach to artistic freedom. When the Swedish MP says she wants to imprison left-wingers, she is most likely telling the truth. But the left-wingers are betraying their honourable tradition. In 2014, Park was arrested during the opening of an exhibit of collage posters. He was also sentenced to six months in prison for incitement to racial agitation and defamation and fined 60,000 kronor in damages to four people who had been displayed on his pictures.[17]

While Park quickly became anathema to the Swedish establishment, he fared better in Denmark, where his fame mainly rested on the intense public debate about freedom of speech that his case had generated. On 23 October, 2014, Parks' nine images previously singled out for destruction were exhibited

The purpose of art **45**

at Christiansborg, the Danish Parliament, as an attempt to raise questions about artistic freedom, but also, perhaps, as a gentle reminder of the political gap between Denmark and Sweden.[18]

When the opportunity arises, positive nationalists use the media, politics and academia to counter dissenting artists. The left will claim this creates an imbalance where the artist is defenceless against a battery of allegations from the establishment. But judging from the cases of Vilks and Park above, history repeated itself. Now, a left-wing entourage to close to mention to the media, the political apparatus, academia, and the courts, were clamping down on rebellious artists. Why didn't these left-wingers defend the defenceless artist against the establishment?

It is now time to turn to the last aspect in this art discussion where similarities between positive and masochist nationalists are being suggested. It has to do with an art expert in court to provide context and to avoid populist verdicts about what the artist "actually means." The Hungarian Ambassador above would most likely oppose the idea. He would claim the Linz Exhibition only had served the purpose of depicting Hungarians as Fascists. What is there to interpret? Left-wingers, then, would insist on an art critic in court. Like Montaigne and to the wild disapproval of conservatives, they would shrug their shoulders, saying no explanation is necessarily better than any other: Who are we to judge? Again, however, their enlightened opinion seems confined to their own ideology of preference, at least if we go by the important case of Dan Park. During the trial against him, no art expert was present, and the prosecutor Linda Rasmussen took the opportunity to inform the court about the "true meaning" of Park's images: A black man was depicted in chains, and therefore Park was a racist. The following dialogue is supposed to have taken place between Rasmussen and Park: R: "Why can't you tell us how your picture should be interpreted?" P: "As an artist? Am I supposed to tell you what to see?" R: "But what are people supposed to think when they see the picture?" P: "Pictures can and must be interpreted in many different ways – or else it is just propaganda!"[19]

Rasmussen's performance did not, however, dissuade the influential curator and art critic above. His verdict may represent Sweden's art scene and cultural establishment: "Are (Park's) pictures contributing to new, experimental (sic!) or broad social discussion," he asked, "or are they rather fuelling a single-minded, unnecessarily insulting, nationalistic and xenophobic agenda?" The curator also deplored the fact that Park had failed to take various measures to ease the pressure, such as "a clarifying article, text messages on the walls in the gallery, press releases, pedagogic gallery tours, or a broadcasted art discussion."[20] What, exactly, was Park supposed to clarify? Park had succeeded provoking a member of the establishment, who now complained saying Park had failed. What would Kurt Weill have done, if German right-wingers had suggested a pedagogic radio discussion could modify his cynicism? From opposite ends, positive and masochist nationalists oppose the idea of artistic freedom because they only defend it when it suits their own ideology.

46 The purpose of art

Notes

1 Ambassador: Cancel provocative Roma art exhibit, 9 October, 2013.
2 Artleaks, 3 October, 2013.
3 Ban art that targets far right, 8 October, 2013.
4 "Fängsla konstnärer som målar könsorgan," 17 June, 2014.
5 Conversation with Park.
6 Elisabeth Höglund, "Lars Vilks missbrukar yttrandefriheten", 25 February, 2013; "Peter Weiderud: Dags att ta avstånd från Vilks hädelser," 14 December, 2010.
7 See, for instance, Edlund, 2018. A shocking account from a woman who became priest because she believed in God, and was harassed for it.
8 "Två partiledare ger Vilks del av skulden," 19 May, 2010.
9 "Gatukonstnären Dan Park döms till fängelse – för hets mot folkgrupp," 8 November, 2018.
10 "Lars Vilks, Gay Mohammed and Freedom of Expression," 2010.
11 "Lars Vilks Rondellhundar: Ett förlöjligande utan syfte," 14 June, 2010; "Ignore Vilks' Muhammad show: religious heads", 26 February, 2013.
12 Orwell, 2001, p. 169.
13 Kristoffer Larsson, "Something is rotten in Sweden," 20 October, 2007.
14 "Vilks kan ju inte rita," 15 March, 2010. While this does not change the discussion in the least, Vilks, in fact, is an accomplished artist. "Vikten av att vara Vilks," SvD, 27 June, 2010.
15 Robert Stasinski, 2014.
16 "Gatukonstnären Dan Park döms till fängelse – för hets mot folkgrupp." SVT Nyheter, 8 November, 2018.
17 Swedish artist jailed for "race hate" pictures, 21 August, 2014; Sentenced: Swedish Artist Dan Park "Incited Against an Ethnic Group," 12 October, 2014.
18 Dan Parks forbudte billeder vises på Christiansborg i dag, 23 October, 2014.
19 Dan Park till åklagaren: Det är ju ni som har svarta på hjärnan!, 3 April, 2019.
20 Robert Stasinski, 2014.

6

THE OGRE OF COLLECTIVISM

Below, we shall discuss three similarities between those two manifestations of nationalism. First, none of them believe in the virtues of equality. Instead, "their side" should be given special attention, whether it relates to employment or public mourning for the dead. Second, "our culture," whether here or elsewhere, is claimed to be the victim of ethnic discrimination, while other categories, such as class, are seen as undermining the conservative pre-eminence of culture. Third, we have the right to impose our values on other cultures, says one, while another says other cultures should feel free to exercise foreign intrusion upon us.

Inequality

Positive nationalists are opposed to equality. Different ethnic groups are treated unequally. The domestic population must be protected by the sole virtue of being "natives," "whites," "Christians," or "Europeans." Foreign job applicants have a lot to prove. We must, positive nationalists maintain, see to ourselves, and uphold a certain quota of indigenous population. At Japanese Universities, 5 per cent are foreigners – at Qatar University in United Arab Emirates even less. Favouring locals like this was common in conservative societies. Then came transparent bureaucracies, and so meritocracy – the law of talent – overtook nepotism, class privileges, and racism. It was a shift of kind, not of degree. But somehow things went too far. Masochist nationalists refused to concede at something as half-hearted and unexciting as an impersonal principle of equal rights. The world had been exploited by the West, and now it was time to set things straight by being equally vindictive from the other end. The ensuing scenario can be illustrated by the concept of "hate crime."

"Hate crime" came into common usage in the United States during the 1980s. It is related to the victim's background and carries a stronger punishment

48 The ogre of collectivism

compared to a crime unrelated to a particular group. For many years, native Swedes were not included in the definition. No matter the weight of the evidence, you could not legally claim a crime against one Swede was due to this person being Swedish. In 2009, however, after considerable pressure by conservatives, attacks against Swedes were also included under the law. But there were barely no practical consequences. In 2013 Susanne Gosenius had started categorised suspicions of hate crime against Swedes and the number was close to zero per year, or about 1/300 reported total hate crimes. No court has ever taken up a case and experts wonder whether it is even worth trying.[1] Two years later, this bias against native Swedes was illustrated twice.

In 2015, two acts of murder made the headlines in Sweden – one on IKEA in Västerås and another one in Trollhättan. In IKEA a man who had just received a negative asylum decision stabbed two Swedish natives to death because, he said: "they looked Swedish." In Trollhättan, a right-wing extremist murdered three immigrants.[2] Both acts appeared as classic hate crimes, but the unfolding events differed greatly. Within days, the Trollhättan killer and his victims became household names. In cities throughout Sweden, a silent minute was held in honour of the assassinated migrants, and in Stockholm, the Social Democrats headed a candle-lit manifestation "Against Racist Violence, and in Defence of Sweden as a Society characterised by Openness and Solidarity." Hundreds of thousands of citizens answered a Facebook call against "Racism and Xenophobia." In Västerås, however, things were quiet. The victims on IKEA remained anonymous. No portraits of a loving mother and son, no personal stories against a backdrop of strings. Even today, few know about Carola and Emil Herlin. The mother, a medical doctor on a short visit to her son – a freshman, both passing by at IKEA to pick up a few kitchen utensils for his new flat. There were no manifestations, no candles, no tens of thousands of grief-struck Swedes throughout the country lining up in collective agony. The Swedish Prime Minister Stefan Löfven had rushed to Trollhättan, but he never visited Västerås. A meaningless, terrible act against non-Swedes had nation-wide repercussion, while an equally pointless act against two Swedes was quickly glossed over almost like an embarrassment. One was deemed hate crime, the other one wasn't despite over-whelming evidence. If these two examples are not isolated events, Sweden is influenced by an attitude whereby non-Swedes systematically are being favoured in relation to native Swedes – i.e. by masochist nationalism.

Positive nationalists use quotas to discriminate against minorities and fill institutions with the majority, while masochist nationalists use quotas to maximise the number of minorities while excluding the majority. One case of inequality is mirrored by another. Workplaces, positive nationalists say, benefit from uniform staff – which is typically racist, say masochist nationalists, claiming "Diversity is enriching." From both manifestations of nationalism, meritocracy is side-lined by partial interest. The historical struggle against class-privileges has left the stage for the benefit of institutionalised inequality and old-school egocentrism. Politicians from one camp say a dead minority teenager sucked in

The ogre of collectivism **49**

in drug-dealing is "just gang-related" as if he is not a human being, while murdered natives cannot quite grasp the attention of politicians from the other camp. They resemble George Orwell's left-wing literary intellectuals of the 1940s who could not help "getting a kick" of their own self-humiliation.

Mystifying ethnic discrimination

Another way of showing this masochist nationalist tendency whereby the unspectacular majority comes out on the losing end is to ask: What is discrimination essentially about? "Nationality and ethnic belonging," says the positive nationalist. Discrimination is always between groups and most importantly against his own proud culture. Discrimination within ethnic groups are liberal and Marxist fiction, because ethnic groups are essentially harmonious. Discrimination between classes based on political or economic factors is overlooked, because it threatens the idea of ethnic concord – a euphemism for conservative elite rule. The positive nationalist is not strong and happy but fragile and aggressive. Any offence hits the entire ethnic group – i.e. is magnified to an act of discrimination against the indigenous majority population. It is one for all, and all for one.

In the eyes of the masochist nationalist, this is all conservative or worse. When discrimination is reduced to ethnicity, other causes for discrimination is forgotten, at least within "our" culture, and masochist nationalists would not hold back their criticism against members of the establishment who would see discrimination as framed by ethnic unity.

But to pass the test of consistency, masochist nationalists must exercise political caution, whereby positive nationalist ethnicity as sole reason behind discrimination is being replaced by a great variety of factors, such as economic, political, social, ethnic/cultural and, of course, individual ones. Neither the majority nor minorities have special favours. Excessive focus on discrimination against the majority leads to oppression of minorities, while uncalled for attention to minorities discriminates – by the same token – against the majority. But, at least judging by the three cases below, masochist nationalists fail this test of consistency. This is all, they believe, a one-sided battle: the stronger the attack against old-school discrimination, the more emancipating the outcome. The first example shows how the majority is trading places as key object of discrimination with various minorities. The second example brings to attention how Swedish authorities, in their energetic quest for inclusion, merely have traded the emotional pre-eminence of the insider with the emotional superiority of the outsider. The third example, finally, will try to show how economic conflict will be disregarded inside of minority communities, evoking memories of class-based discrimination in yesterday's Europe. In all these cases, masochist nationalists exercise no political caution, and their efforts will only reinforce positive nationalist's discriminatory practise – only on behalf of overseas' cultures.

Diskrimineringsombudsmannen (DO) stands for the official Swedish bureau against discrimination. Few countries have more thoroughly done away with

50 The ogre of collectivism

ethnic obsession positive nationalist style. Therefore, in case an all-inclusive definition of discrimination would exist at all, it ought to be found at DO. Their homepage, however, tells a different story. It refers to "seven grounds for discrimination covered by law. These are: 'gender,' 'gender transgressing identity or expression,' 'ethnic belonging,' 'religion or other belief,' 'handicap,' 'sexual predisposition' and 'age.'" The tendency towards identity politics is clear, and only two grounds – age and handicap – includes the majority. And discrimination based on political factors is absent, even though, historically, this is what discrimination was often about.[3] In case you suffer from political discrimination, DO offers no help.

The difference between positive nationalist old-style discrimination and this supposedly progressive definition on the homepage of DO is hard to see. While positive nationalists are obsessed by alleged discrimination against an indigenous ethnic majority, masochist nationalists seem equally compelled by supposed acts of discrimination against minorities, particularly ethnic minorities. In a previous discussion about political representation based on ethnic belonging, it was argued that this is likely to turn ethnic representatives into semi-gods with no political accountability, much like "charismatic" right-wing populist leaders spending their time shaking hands instead of engaging in political affairs. The present discussion is another case in point. Neither positive nationalism nor discrimination along the lines of DO acknowledge discrimination on economic and political grounds, the reason being, possibly, because economic and political justice is bound to foster social change. Instead, in line with conservative rhetoric, ethnicity is hailed as supreme line of demarcation. Ethnicity trumps politics – a platitude among conservatives but a sensation among left-wingers. For all its progressive aura, this latter version of discrimination fits into a masochist nationalist programme. The majority is never in the right and discrimination against it is not important. Discrimination mostly occurs within the majority, but this is discarded for ideological reasons. Minorities, masochist nationalists feel, are constantly subject to our structural discrimination, and as they acknowledge this, they sense that enticing mix of paper-thin shame and elevation – a pastime activity among the select few who can toy with disgrace and fragility, turn suffering into aesthetics, and who know pride and calls for vengeance – values they happily assign to others – is the mark of the destitute. The dubious might of the majority has been replaced by the dubious might of the minority. In this scheme, there is little room for the bland indigenous population, often with no other cause for discrimination than economic abuse and political harassing. Quoting David Bromwich, Kenan Malik writes thus: "Indeed, so deeply attached" is this "idea of cultural, as opposed to economic or political justice, that David Bromwich is led to wonder whether intellectuals today would oppose economic slavery if it lacked any racial or cultural dimension."[4] With one striking image, Bromwich captures the intellectual collapse of masochist nationalism. There are two types of conservatives ignoring economic exploitation for the benefit of ethnic unity – positive nationalists and masochist nationalists.

The ogre of collectivism **51**

Our second example will try to show how Swedish authorities, in their anti-discriminatory endeavours, only replace the supremacy of the insider with the pre-eminence of the outsider. In 2009, an unemployed Muslim man met a female company representative. He was enrolled at the State Employment Agency and had applied for job training at the company. During the interview, he refused to shake hands, and his unemployment pay was terminated. He took it to court and received 60,000 Swedish Kronor in damages. "I am relieved," Katri Linna, then head of Diskrimineringsombudsmannen (DO) announced, "that the court makes it clear that the decision made by State Employment Agency is unacceptable in our Swedish multi-religious society."[5] Fortunately, we have long since stopped giving special favours to Swedes. But wasn't this actually more of the same? The person who had refused to shake hands was the man, not the woman. You simply can't work here, the company had insisted, unless you accept our social rules, but their plea was ignored. DO sided with the man's subjective account, and his economic destitution, if anything, spoke in his favour. Why was the woman's perspective overlooked? After all, the interview took place in Sweden where people shake hands. It was overlooked, probably, because she belonged to a White, Christian majority.

What if the man had claimed ethnic discrimination under nationalist flag – in Thailand, for instance? If he had forced himself into some important government office in one of those over-sized compounds in the outskirts of Bangkok, and you can only speculate, those around him might have looked at him for a moment in silence. Then his claims would have been dismissed. On a good day it would only be an amusing interruption. Still, he'd be sentenced to pay damages to the woman and, perhaps, for failing to adhere to Thai customs and for being a troublemaker, and so on. A similar biased verdict would have come out of it, but the damages and the state's response would instead have been resolutely in favour of the woman and not in favour of the man. If the scenario seems ominous, the masochist nationalist reality above is no less politically disconcerting, even though it is not quite seen as such.

We now turn to a third example of how the discussion around discrimination has shifted from an obsession with the wrongdoings against "our" ethnicity to alleged abuses against the ethnicity of "others." It is taken from an interview in Swedish television in 2016.[6] The example shows how the notion of economic and political discrimination is pushed aside for the benefit of a mystical idea of a unified ethnic minority. A young female journalist interviewed a government employee in her spacious Stockholm office – both with a background in the same Middle Eastern country. "So, the journalist finally asked, what's your salary?" "98,000." "But… don't you think that's a lot?" The lady behind the desk snapped: "No, I want more!" The journalist hesitated, as if the old idea of economic injustice still resonated faintly inside her. Then, she pulled herself together encouraged, presumably, by their shared identity. The success of the elegant, outspoken lady was also the fortune of a young, underpaid journalist. They both smiled and back in the studio the TV-host was also smiling.

52 The ogre of collectivism

While high-paid positive nationalists in the past had little sense of community, a similar behaviour in the face of a struggling European journalist would be hard to find today. Why? Because history has taught us that sentimental rhetoric about our common fate is upper-class manipulation to retain class privileges. Cultural unity is code word for economic oppression. Still, the same sentimental rhetoric has been brought back again, surprisingly, by its previous left-wing censors. While these sentiments are no longer possible to apply on their own country for reasons of career and public reputation, masochist nationalists have retreated to a second line of defence and started endorsing upper-class arrogance inside of exotic cultures with no sense of inner contradiction. Since they are, after all, deeply romantic neo-leftists, they are far more enticed by images of vengeance and greatness overseas than by worker's rights in Iran. Therefore, they pack all those frustrated reactionary emotions in a suitcase, embark on an intercontinental flight and unpack it on an exotic shore where the entire bandwidth of radical conservatism come flying out – collectivism, repression of the individual, lofty utopianism and political manipulation, and – of course – class hatred from above; all risk-free and exciting because the geographical setting where they perform these dark rituals has been the victim of "European colonialism."

But what about the young journalist? Whether ethnic discrimination is applied to a nation in the West or to a foreign country, those likely to profit from it are the select few on top. Not only was the journalist forced to endure a shameless upper-class fellow citizen, she was also subject to disrespect by the TV-host and the viewers, but also trained and taught to take pleasure in her own deprivation. In many ways, it resembled a 19th-century scene before the rise of liberalism and socialism. No matter if this class-based humiliation comes from Westerners waving their own flags, or rather from Western patrons waving flags from overseas, they both belong to the same basket of arrogance from above.

And if you cannot expect an underpaid journalist to feel happy on behalf of an insatiable government employee, why would someone on the other end of the social ladder be any more faithful in the opposite direction, just because it would fit into the exotifying scheme of a masochist nationalist? Daiva Stasiulis has written about the Pakistani immigrant community in Canada. Why, she wonders, must a Canadian MP from Lahore always act on behalf of her fellow citizens? Why would Pakistani culture come on top of shared beliefs along other lines – such as class and cultural taste?[7] Masochist nationalists all know about Pierre Bourdieu and the attraction of social classes, but regarding exotic countries it is as if he never existed.

A Bureau of Discrimination with only two grounds covering ethnic minorities would be hard to defend. A mere two grounds relating to the rights of the majority is even more surprising. From opposite ends, positive nationalists and masochist nationalists are mystifying ethnic discrimination on behalf of their respective culture of esteem. When two cultural systems of social greetings collide, the customs of the country should prevail, but no one should pay damages. From the heights of their towers, positive nationalists used to expect domestic

The ogre of collectivism **53**

workers to welcome upper-class greed. Today, masochist nationalists expect poor migrant journalists to welcome minority upper-class greed, and also when the elites in return pretend to give up any upper-class social allegiances for the benefit of a misty "shared background." Positive nationalists, worth adding, always used to feed the lower classes with the very same empty promises.

Foreign intrusion

As part of early 20th-century imperialism, Western empires forced legislation on overseas cultures. The Anarchical and Revolutionary Crimes Act of 1919, better known as the Rowlatt Act, for instance, authorised British government in India to imprison anyone suspected for "terrorism" for two years without a trial.[8] Below, a few cases of foreign intrusion will be discussed. It will be claimed that masochist nationalists, despite their reputation as being on the side of non-interventionism and pacifism in general, see no problem with foreign intrusion against a sovereign nation as long as it suits their ideological agenda. Their campaigning against positive nationalist' intrusion, then, is cast in doubt. They don't mind intrusion, it seems, but they do mind the West. Finally, we shall briefly discuss the theory of sanctions. This theory questions the principles behind foreign intrusion in any direction and may offer a more lasting defence of the idea of national sovereignty.

Positive nationalists never shy away from imposing their values on foreign cultures. Their own values, on the other hand, tower above any criticism. It is all one-sided and parochial. We have a lot to offer you, but you have nothing to offer us. The natural response, then, it to follow some principle of autonomy. Every nation has the right to self-protection. But if you merely start protecting the sovereignty of other cultures while ignoring the autonomy of your own, you are only doing more of the same thing. This would characterise a masochist nationalist, copying, in fact supporting and strengthening the romantic, self-eulogising practise of his right-wing adversaries under the mistaken assumption of doing the opposite. Other cultures have a lot to offer us, but we have nothing to offer other cultures.

Perhaps the best example of this masochist nationalist mirror image of positive nationalism is the ways in which the political Islamic doctrine – including Sharia laws – is spreading in the West. From their strongholds in academia, media and party politics, masochist nationalists have supported Muslim attempts to impose the doctrine of political Islam throughout the Western community. But what is this doctrine about? Is it compatible with Western values? Ayaan Hirsi Ali, prominent critic of Islam, is pessimistic about it:

> If you get deep into the values and the principles that are promoted from within the political Islamic doctrine, and you put them next to our Western political ideas, you get to a place of a zero-sum games. No society can be both. The contemporary Western mind is taught to collaborate, to

54 The ogre of collectivism

> cooperate, to compromise – pluralism, tolerance, all to me fantastic ideas
> and a fantastic attitude towards the world. But sometimes you get to a place
> where it is impossible to compromise.

She touches upon one of the pillars of liberalism: To what extent should we compromise with those who chose not to? "Sharia is one of the oldest political philosophies in the world." she continues, and it is not meant as a compliment. It "does not make sense to the Western mind."[9] I am a Swede living in Amman, Jordan, and the two countries are on opposite ends of the World Value Survey. There are hundreds of young girls in Jordanian prisons, but not to be punished but to be protected.

Our eagerness to combine two incompatible systems shows two things. First, masochist nationalists are not guided by reason: If so, they would agree with Hirsi Ali: No society can be both. Instead, they are influenced by emotions, and that sentiment addressed by George Orwell long ago: "Our own country must be in the wrong." The West must greatly benefit from the Islamic political doctrine, and if not, the fault is ours.

Second, we are again reminded of George Orwell. Even though a Catholic and a Communist, he says, say different things, "from the point of view of an outsider, they are very much alike."[10] As a principle, the masochist nationalist and his carelessness about his own country to the point where he would let it be influenced by a brutal, alien religious doctrine is no different from the Rowlett Act and similar ways in which positive nationalists always imposed their customs and laws on foreign cultures.

One may of course replace old school proselytising overseas with a self-humiliating proselytising in the opposite direction. It is possible the way one may slander one's own church, culture, food, language and history, while feeling excited at the sight of the very same things abroad. But this has nothing to do with the abstract idea that foreign intrusion is bad. And it also means that one's widely announced anti-nationalism is only a facade.

Two recent examples shall end the discussion about how these two nationalists alternate between condemning foreign intrusion and insisting on it: the NATO bombings of Serbia during the spring of 1999, and the EU sanctions in early 2000 against the Austrian government coalition between the People's Party and Jörg Haider's Freedom Party. Is it allowed to punish a sovereign state for a supposedly higher cause? And how do you justify it? As we shall see, political principles give no guidance. Instead, it all goes back to ideological self-interest. In the eyes of an old-school nationalist, the NATO bombings against communist Serbia were justified. At the time, communists were the exotic "Others." more so, in fact, than Kosovo Muslims. Besides, it would teach Serbia a lesson, and support for nationalist movements would diminish when Belgrade was bombarded. Sanctions against Austria, on the other hand, were not justified. Besides, they were counterproductive, because they would only fuel support for Jörg Haider and Austrian far-right wingers. Foreign intrusion was both good and bad.

Masochist nationalists saw it from the other end. The NATO bombings did not have UN Security Council support and constituted a violation against international law. The political scheme where communists were abandoned for the benefit of cultures overseas, such as in Afghanistan, had not yet materialised. On top of it, the bombings would fuel nationalist sentiments and support for Slobodan Milošević. The sanctions against Austria, on the other hand, were justified. When the Belgian Foreign Minister Louis Michel declared skiing in Austria "immoral." and a delegation of Austrian students at a European-wide youth event in Strasbourg were castigated as "Nazis" as they mounted the stage, it would all teach Austrians a lesson and they would stop supporting Jörg Haider.[11] Foreign intervention was both good and bad.

It is hard to make sense of this based on the principle of non-intervention, because neither positive nor masochist nationalists seem to have a clear opinion about it. But if you instead see it from the point of view of ideological self-interest while trying to keep your head above water on the higher principle of national sovereignty, the behaviour is easier to understand. "Enlightened opinion," George Orwell said, is often conservative rhetoric upturned. On a Monday, they are pacifists, and on a Wednesday, they are warmongers.[12] To old-school nationalists, Haider was a champion of the West and his critics were self-abasing multiculturalists and left-wingers. Therefore, the EU-sanctions against Austria were called a "violation against free and fair elections." To masochist nationalists, NATO was an emblematic exponent of the US and the West. Consequently, the NATO attacks were described as "a violation against a sovereign state" – while the sovereignty of Austria was unimportant because Jörg Haider was a "right-wing extremist."

There seems to be no way out. But instead of oscillating from one extreme to another, there is a middle ground that may offer an escape from this nationalist impasse. It is related to the theory of sanctions – a classic case of foreign intervention. How is a country affected by sanctions? The answers may suggest a principled approach beyond ideological conflicts and partial interests.

Why are sanctions implemented? Often to punish or seek compliance, or both. Even if there is no compliance, there is still, Johan Galtung comments, "at least the gratification that derives from knowing (or believing) that the sinner gets his due, that the criminal has been punished."[13] Sanctions, he continues, have less to do with any effects in the country under attack than on hoped-for appreciation among voters back home.

Do sanctions work? A 1971 study showed only 20 percent of all sanctions were effective.[14] According to an eight-country study from the 1960s, around 25 per cent were effective, and a 1990 investigation indicates about 5 per cent brought about political compliance.[15] A punishment against a collective "will always," Galtung maintains, "affect the just together with the unjust, since collective sanctions correspond to a philosophy of collective guilt," which, of course violates the modern mind. In case the sanctioned country is seen as an "undifferentiated whole," this holistic image will immediately be exploited by the countries'

56 The ogre of collectivism

right-wingers.[16] According to the scientific rule of thumb, sanctions are at best ineffective, often counterproductive.

If masochist nationalists believe right-wing unification against foreign intrusion only occurs when they find the aggressor politically unappealing – NATO for instance – they should explain why this is so. Unless they do, their calls for foreign intrusion – and non-intervention when it suits them – are indistinguishable from the haphazard policy of positive nationalists, even though the political tension in the West might be summed up by the hostility between them. The problem is not ideological convictions. We all have them. The problem is when political principles are wiped aside for the benefit of ideological convictions. If sanctions can tell us anything about the general effects of foreign intrusion, both positive and nationalists appear to be mistaken when they insist on collective punishment against a sovereign country.

Notes

1 "Polisen: Offer väljs ut för att de är svenskar," 13 March, 2016.
2 Mördarens val av offer: "De såg svenska ut," 21 October, 2015.
3 Om Diskrimineringsombudsmannen.
4 Kenan Malik, "Against Multiculturalism."
5 Ledare: Kärnvärdena gäller alla.
6 The sources have asked to remain anonymous.
7 Stasiulis, 2002.
8 Vohra, p. 126.
9 Ayaan Hirsi Ali on the West, Dawa and Islam.
10 Orwell, 2001, p 169.
11 Adamson, 2016b, p. 16.
12 Orwell, 1945.
13 Galtung, 1967, p. 380.
14 Wallensteen, 1971, p. 166.
15 Galtung, 1967, p. 382; Pape, 1997, p. 93.
16 Galtung, 1967, p. 409.

7

POWER AND EMOTIONS

Power and emotions

In a scene in Anton Chekov's *The Cherry Orchard*, a young man comes running onto the stage. At the sight of him, Mademoiselle Ranevsky, the orchard owner, bursts out in tears. He had been present years ago when her son Grisha drowned and now it all comes back to her. Her sister is upset: "But I told you, Peter, to wait till tomorrow!" "My Grisha... my boy... Grisha... my son," the woman sobs. Who is to blame? The young man? Clearly, he was the trigger. But was he also the culprit? Shouldn't Mademoiselle Ranevsky after all those years handle the sight of him?

The discussion above has tried to display a number of key features of positive nationalism. The individual is a mere bolt in the nationalist project, its culture is revered beyond reason, and history books are turned into state propaganda. The scene in Chekov's play illustrates another aspect in the nationalist toolkit: might is right – and might infused by emotions is even better. Mademoiselle Ranevsky was an aristocrat – in tears at that.

An argument, Chekov seems to say, should be assessed on its own merit. Your social standing and your emotions changes nothing. Positive nationalists, however, always said those in power are right, and a proper display of emotions could always support the case. Critics from the crowds below were dismissed as far-left demagogues undermining society, and in the face of these exercises of social control workers often remained silent. But after the Second World War and the welfare state on the rise, class-privileges fell in disrepute. Chekov's suggestion to disregard social standing and emotions was gaining ground. Gradually, however, masochist nationalists started seeing these progressive ideas as too much of a compromise. The only radical response, they felt, was to turn the old power game against the West and to give the upper hand to minorities, the more upset,

58 Power and emotions

the better. Three examples will illustrate what happened when the outdated scheme of privileges reappeared with the coat inside out.

Above, we saw how a Muslim man had refused to shake hands with a female company manager. As the sky cleared, he had received 60 000 Swedish kronor in damages. Unfair treatment of minorities had been replaced by unfair treatment of the majority. Here, we are chiefly interested in the fact that not only was he portrayed as powerless, but his response, along with groups and organisations supporting him, were highly emotional. The court had been taken in by their vividly displayed disapproval, and the man's status as jobless migrant was, if anything, counting in his favour. Chekov's upper-class lady in tears had returned in the shape of an aggrieved and supposedly subjugated Muslim man.

After centuries of struggle, modern, impartial jurisdiction arose and managed to replace conservative supremacy, where subjective accounts had an unreasonable impact on the verdict. Now, masochist nationalists were eager to take one step further – or rather back – and have modern jurisdiction replaced by subjective supremacy of those deemed powerless – a strong counter-measure against old-school injustice but a poor defence of impartial rights.

The unfolding events after the infamous Mohammed cartoons in 2005 offer another illustration, where all those nationalist visions of power and raging emotions were brought back in the hands of a supposed underdog. First, however, one should not forget that caricatures and cartoons were always looked upon with suspicion by positive nationalists as well. A famous case where a right-wing power elite clamped down on left-wing caricatures took place in France in the early 1830s. In 1831, the leading French satirical publication La Caricature published "Gargantua" – a caricature depicting an over-sized Louis Philippe devouring all the goods of the poor, while excreting gifts and honours to his corrupt aristocratic supporters. As a result, La Caricature was convicted twice, its editor jailed for one year, and the caricaturist himself for five months – a classic case of positive nationalist display of excessive power from above.[1]

But back to the Mohammed cartoons. Their publication in the Danish newspaper *Jyllands-Posten* sparked massive demonstrations in the Muslim world. People were killed, Danish flags were torched, and the boycott's price tag in lost export revenues to the Muslim world exceeded one billion Danish kronor. In the West, the events caused widespread confusion. One could have questioned whether the reactions were in proportion to a caricature on paper. But instead, fuelled by post-colonial guilt and multicultural enthusiasm for all things exotic, this collective rage from underneath could not possibly, it was felt, be exaggerated. Instead, it was appropriate and just – a mere mirror image of the unspeakable insult of the cartoons. The political rule of thumb – only listen to those who can present a coherent argument – had been upturned, and many Western commentators could barely hide their enthusiasm at the sight of these religious fanatics from overseas. The supremacy of power had been replaced by the rule of the powerless. Watching the unfolding of the massive demonstrations, journalists, academics and politicians gradually came to understand just how offensive the cartoons had been. We had it coming. Not only could they enjoy the chilling satisfaction of pleasure in pain, but they also came to realise, or so they thought, that fury was the only evidence of despair.

Still, these reactions say nothing about whether the cartoons should have been published or not. Emotions have no impact on the content of an argument, whether it comes from an orchard owner above or a raging crowd from below. The only thing we know when people are angry is that they are angry. When the West sided with agitated Muslims and tore apart a cartoonist and a Danish quality newspaper, we furnished Islam with an authoritarian idea that used to belong to the upper-class in the West: Truth comes with fury. Intellectuals talk too much. Violence or the threat of it carries its own justification. In TV-studios, journalists could barely hide their arousal, and the air was heavy with fascism – at least in theory. When millions of Muslims felt humiliated, our scepticism went missing, and masochist nationalists gazed at them with that chilling mix of reverence and distant curiosity. Not long ago, all of this political romanticism had justified atrocities against others. Now, the same ideas had turned against the West.

Above, we touched upon an event from France during the 1830s to give perspective from the camp of positive nationalists. But to illustrate the full force of the Islamist response to the cartoons, we might suggest a corresponding reaction from the European right. Caricatures mocking Muhammed would cause tremendous unease in Muslim communities, but even the slightest concern would be deemed out-of-proportion and an insult, while any action on our side was to be expected. They had it coming. We would smile and shake our head at the sight of these exotic individuals who seem not to understand there are limits to everything, and some of us would watch our uniformed fanatics in TV-studios, announcing we will now engage in massive retaliation, so can't they see how right we are? This is a highly disconcerting scenario with fascist overtones. Still, it is the same violent manifestation of emotions and power, this time, only, from above in the service of positive nationalists.

We used to justify our own brutality with romantic determinism – we were provoked and "acted accordingly" – a pet phrase among Marxists and Fascists not long ago. Now, frustrated over the fact that it is no longer possible to fill our own actions with lack-of-choice grandeur because people we depend on would not allow it, masochist nationalists have found another outlet for all their craving after Dionysian greatness and sacrifice, and against that accursed liberal individual autonomy – all in theory of course because in practice they don't mind independence at all. When they see Islamists bursting with fresh and exciting fury against us, these Islamists bring to life all that stifled lust for proto-fascist entertainment so common among masochist nationalists, and when this entertainment goes under the name of cultural sensitivity, it is an opportunity not to be missed. While positive nationalists may relinquish their own autonomy to excuse atrocities overseas, masochist nationalists may deprave the Other of free choice to excuse terror in Paris, Brussels and elsewhere.

60 Power and emotions

The case of suicide bombers offers a third and final example of this upturned power mystique. In the eyes of masochist nationalists, a suicide bomber is the image of the powerless, despite their powerful intentions. If an argument is fortified by emotions, no amount of knowledge strengthens your case more than a suicide attack. Regarding exotic cultures, our ignorance allows us to dwell in poetic idealizations about their reactions and attitudes; and the more ridiculous, extreme, and bizarre, the more inspiring, bold, and majestic. Their submissiveness to a final cause is a sign of greatness and purpose, while our own liberal independence makes everything aimless and primitive like beasts living hand-to-mouth. From a masochist nationalist point of view, the autonomy of modernity appears erratic and backward, while lack of free choice evokes creativity and modernity. The keywords are self-annihilation and utopianism, to be admired only, of course, in the service of overseas' cultures – which is also what a positive nationalist would admire, but only in case the same violent utopianism is drummed up on behalf of his own culture.

Regarding suicide bombers, the gramophone of power is turning backwards. Now, social control is exercised from "below," and those above may choose to remain silent to avoid accusations for being – not revolutionaries and extreme left-wingers – but extreme right-wingers and racists seeking to destabilise society.

The political project of powerlessness is a handmaiden to oppression and conservatism, despite its aura of socialism and anti-authority. It is laden with power-mysticism, although this mysticism is not about power, but about powerlessness. Positive nationalists say your argument has power because you are powerful. Masochist nationalists, sentimentally, claim it has power because you are powerless. There is little support for these ideas in socialist tradition, however. Karl Marx told the powerless not to seek power through self-pity and by embracing powerlessness. Instead, they should seek power, knowledge and influence by their own effort. Feeling excluded only asks for upper-class pity. "We have no compassion," Marx wrote in *Neue Rheinische Zeitung*, "and we ask no compassion from you."[2] The essence of powerlessness is not knowledge but lack of it. This sentimental attitude towards powerlessness was always a safe option for any arrogant elite seeking to keep the underclass in a state of blissful ignorance – and being admired for it. Yesterday, positive nationalists spared a penny for the homeless and had social stability in return, and today, masochist nationalists are full of pity for powerless migrants, who respond with gratitude, as the powerless always did faced with upper-class manipulation.

A further link between them emerges. We do not notice the powerless because they lack power. Those who really can tell the story of Gulag are no longer with us, Alexander Solzhenitsyn once remarked, "The truly powerless are absent. We pay attention when they exercise power. It is not their fragility that makes us weary, but their fury." As noted by Bruce Bawer, "There are people in China and India and South America who are far poorer than most Islamist terrorists but who would never do such things."[3] At this point, we have come full circle;

rage makes the supposed powerless powerful. Nationalism is always the tool of the powerful.

The idea of power, masochist nationalists' claim, has been tainted by National Socialism. Therefore, they claim powerlessness is tolerant and "anti-racist." If power was rightist, reactionary and irrational, powerlessness was leftist, progressive and based on reason. Those who exercised power were also said to be the domestic Western majority while exotic minorities were "powerless." What, then, would be better than to side with a powerless, ethnic community?

But the reason why masochist nationalists saw powerlessness as a tropical mirage was not because the philosophical underpinnings of powerlessness were different to the underpinnings of power, but because they were similar. While siding with the views of the powerless could satisfy masochist nationalists' need for public approval as decent left-wingers, it also appealed to their frustrated cravings for primitivism and irrationalism. The views of the powerless are not blurred by knowledge. They are not fooled by temptations of worldly success. The life of the powerless is not decadent, but spiritually rich. Suffering ennobles. The powerless is an ascetic, and his humiliation purifies the soul and enlivens the spirits. Western indecisiveness is traded for Eastern certainty: "You know who you are, and you know what you want." The truly powerless are content, while lack of contentment fuels desires – yet another anti-Western remark as dissatisfaction leads to development and progress. Scarcity sharpens your senses, and you battle with nothing but your naked body. You sense the futility of life on earth, and the joys of the here-after. The above ideas – Rousseauan primitivism, Tolstoian asceticism, Eastern dogmatism, and Gandhian utopianism, are important for anyone who finds powerlessness virtuous and enchanting.

The philosophical underpinnings of powerlessness are impossible to imagine within a rationalist and modernist framework. Whether you idealise power or the lack of it you shun knowledge in its own right. Cult of power as well as cult of powerlessness are both saturated with political romanticism. The masochist nationalist pretends to fight against National Socialism, but his conclusions are anything but mainstream. This, I believe, further strengthens the idea that masochist nationalism and positive nationalism are merely two branches on the nationalist tree.

While seeking to protect ethnic minorities against abusive Europeans, the masochist nationalist will only bring back the old ghosts of positive nationalism: the exotic native as predetermined automat, communities overseas as ethnic zoos, and the West in full control. While the masochist nationalist finds an outlet for his back-pocket need for exciting determinism and soldier morality by depriving individuals overseas of freedom of choice, the positive nationalist finds the same outlet at home. Whether they freely display it in their own country or carry it in a suitcase and unpack it overseas, they are both, says Orwell, absorbed "by hierarchies," and by heroism, blind obedience, and cultural clashes.

The masochist nationalist also prefers aggression to reason as a basis for an argument, embraces any violence seeking the culprit elsewhere, and holds the tradition of the enlightenment in contempt. To the masochist nationalist as well as for the positive nationalist, fury contains its own justification because fury must be caused by an external defamation. They should have known, says one nationalist, or we should have known, says another. The stronger the reaction, the stronger the initial violation: a blend of Marxist determinism and Fascist cult of violence. Both manifestations of nationalism are mesmerised by power and emotions, and none of them acknowledge the virtues of the argument as such and the prospects of gaining new knowledge for free. On the issue of power and emotions, there are many similarities between positive nationalism and masochist nationalism.

Notes

1 Goldstein, 1989, pp. 133–41.
2 Karl Marx, 1849.
3 Bawer, 2006, p. 179.

8

ON MORAL SHOW-OFF AND THE HIDDEN BENEFITS OF SELF-ABASEMENT

In this chapter, we will discuss a common attitude in any fringe ideology, namely societal pessimism. Whether this pessimism is due to dangerous strangers or dangerous natives, it is an important trait in both positive and masochist nationalism. After that, we shall address how both types of nationalist eventually end up in a surprisingly similar heartless, ungenerous attitude towards suffering individuals in overseas' cultures.

Pessimism

The reason why positive nationalists are constantly on guard is because, they sense, they live in hostile surroundings. They feel threatened and must engage in various pre-emptive measures, such as boosting up the war machinery, unite by means of ethnic propaganda, and keep a strict border between ethnic insiders and outsiders. We, they insist, are threatened by them. There is no individual left in this scheme. An offence committed by any non-native is an act by his entire ethnic community against our entire domestic ethnic community. This is the pessimistic mind-set of a positive nationalist.

For most of us, however, the political situation between ethnic groups in Europe is not as bleak as positive nationalists assume. Clearly, recent large-scale migration is weighing heavily on the social systems, in particularly in Sweden and Germany, and crime rate has gone up. Still, positive nationalists always exaggerate, as if pessimism is more exciting and interesting than reality. Besides, statistical material about the relation between crime rates and ethnic belonging is freely available and should dissuade anyone who seeks to whip up nightmarish fantasies. Then again, positive nationalists were never interested in statistics. Pessimistic images, instead, might give them special favours such as an excuse to take to the streets. They can't do anything, they complain, and so they do

64 Moral show-off; self-abasement

everything. Self-pity often comes with self-haughtiness. Positive nationalists invent a threat in order to strike against any group at their own discretion. As a result of this self-pitying pessimism, positive nationalists can no longer take a critical remark for what it is. Instead, they find it offensive, and try to shut down discussions by making criticism illegal. This does not go unnoticed among masochist nationalists. With great zest, they take apart positive nationalists' pessimistic fantasies.

Before trying to answer exactly what this "great zest" means, the question is: What is the proper response to this irrational pessimism whereby your own culture constantly is wrapped up in self-gratifying rhetoric? Presumably rationalism and pragmatism, and self-criticism against romantic notions about one's own infallibility. Act of violence are rarely a clash between ethnic blocks. Generally – and positive nationalists would grit their teeth – it is a conflict confined to a few individuals. There is nothing majestic about it, and the stew is too thin to justify collectivist aggression. And what about defamation, abuse, insults, and blasphemy – all of those nationalist cries of maltreatment that always comes along with a pessimistic, self-aggrandising outlook? It should be countered by pointing out that any political movement is positioned on the scale of left and right and will always be subject to criticism. If they insist criticism against them should be prohibited, they only tell us they are unfit to live in a modern society. Instead of immature calls of "ill-treatment." these critical claims should be met with counter arguments. We should always be thankful to the critic, J.S. Mill noted long ago. Either, he is wrong, and we had to find out, or he is right, and we have to change our mind.

But masochist nationalists are not convinced by this sober attitude, because it does not, they feel, go far enough. The political pessimism surrounding positive nationalism is simply so repulsive any cautious and intellectual response, in fact anything but a whole-sale attack, is a betrayal. A few examples will illustrate the counter-reaction chosen by masochist nationalists.

Positive nationalists, it was noted above, are not interested in crime statistics. They have eyes to see with and they simply know "how bad it is." The crime rate for migrants, for instance, is sky-high, and you don't need data for it. These ideas are easily accessible on alternative media and on right-wing party websites. But masochist nationalists rarely use data to refute these rumours. They simply know migrant crime rate is low. Protocols are forged, court proceedings discriminate against migrants, and research shows that the police force and the legal system are structurally racist. Universities are biased against non-Europeans, the business world is racist, and crime rate among natives is played down because media is racist.[1]

As a consequence of masochist nationalist "great zest," they swiftly move from one corner to another. Instead of relying on data, they replace one conceited pessimism with another. While the positive nationalists, without the support of statistics, say we are threatened by them, the masochist nationalists, equally untroubled by facts, maintain they are threatened by us. Everything is

Moral show-off; self-abasement **65**

negated, and nothing is achieved. Behind the garb of radical rhetoric, Wolfgang Kowalsky claims, multicultural self-harassment is revealed as a "simple strategy whereby problems related to foreigners are being dismissed and belittled." The pessimistic views of the positive nationalist is merely negated: The xenophobes fuel attractive horror scenarios about migrants, while foreigners are being "beautified" by the xenophiles.[2] Among the left, he continues, "it is common to make a distinction between foreigners = victims and Germans = perpetrators."[3] This is all purely emotional, a self-abusing mirror image of positive nationalist self-pity.

When the German author Bernt Engelmann in a TV talk show explained that the crime rate among foreigners is lower than that of the Germans, he is actually, Kowalsky argues, using "counter factual reasoning." Criticism against foreigners, he continues, "is sacrilegious," leaving no other option than to "adjust unpleasant facts in the service of The Truth."[4] The sexual assaults throughout Germany during New Year's Eve 2016 is a good case in point. When the figures finally had been established, more than 2,000 sexual assaults and robberies had taken place, of which 1,529 in Köln, and 236 in Hamburg.[5] Five women had been raped. The number of perpetrators was more than 2,000, and they were practically only men of "Arab or North African appearance." As the New Year dawned, Kowalsky's predictions came true. German Police suddenly experienced difficulties in reporting what had happened, and left-wing media argued that what had happened hadn't actually happened, really, and that, if it had happened, it was just like any Octoberfest in Munich anyway. Why should we point fingers at poor Muslim migrants, when mass rapes against women were ingrained in German culture? The wheels of whitewash were spinning. Not many noticed that the incidents, in the Arab World, were known as Taharrush gamea, "group sexual harassment in crowds." Recently, figures presented by the Swedish Crime Prevention Agency showed that every third woman in the country feels insecure in public, and more than every tenth decides to stay at home. "These figures," says Erik Wennerström, Head of Crime Prevention Agency at the time, are alarming," but "what exactly to do about it, I really don't know."[6] But there is actually available data about it. Over the last few years, Sweden has experienced numerous attacks against women, including rape and sexual abuse either by gangs or single individuals, and young men from Somalia and the Middle East are significantly overrepresented. Perhaps Wennerström had been influenced by a statement by Feminist Initiative – a Swedish political party: "Swedish men may well be No. 1 in the world in terms of harassment and violence against women."[7] These examples illustrate that self-abusive "negative" nationalism and pessimism George Orwell had in mind 80 years ago. It is not true, but feel free to say it.

If positive nationalists are active manufacturing views and sentiments whereby the indigenous population in Europe is under siege by criminal foreign gangs, they are as efficient in depicting cities overseas as hazardous. After the Bali bombings in 2002, many saw the Indonesian capital of Jakarta as dominated

66 Moral show-off; self-abasement

by Islamist. In reality, Jakarta is a safe mega-city of extreme commercialism and Islam light. Amman, capital of Jordan at the heart of the Middle East bordering on Syria to the north, is safer at night than many European cities. Positive nationalist pessimistic images of overseas' countries only reveal they have not travelled and instead they invent racist stereotypes of the local population. Why pay a visit if you already know?

Turning to the perspective of the masochist nationalists, their vision is an upturned replica of the images above. As a matter of fact, geographical home bashing has become an academic field of its own. In a book ominously entitled *The Return of the Führer*, Sweden is brought up as a chilling case: "The same features that characterise the anti-urbane suburbs of (.) Malmö," is no less valid for the "illusionary idylls of the south Swedish province."[8] As a Swede, the authors' views are hard to understand. I assume they want to sell a book to likeminded by evoking feelings of insecurity and violence against immigrants by native Swedes. But the statement is only masochist nationalism on auto-pilot. There are no "illusionary" idylls in the south-Swedish provinces. These areas are rather wealthy, air is fresh, and people are friendly. This does not change just because authors with a flair for pessimistic insinuations say something different. South-Swedish provinces are close to real idylls.

The authors probably never visited these "illusionary idylls" in the first place, because they don't think they have to. Why go there if you already know? South-Swedish provinces, they say, are infested by racism and readers are expected to be aroused by comparing their own country unfavourably to other countries. If they ever saw Amman or Jakarta, you would ask those positive nationalists to show the street thugs and the no go-zones. And where, you'd like to ask a masochist nationalist, are these illusive South-Swedish suburbs and the trampling jackboots? Positive nationalism feeds on ignorance about overseas cultures plus a boy-scout fascination for scary things, and masochist nationalists suppress the little they know about the Scandinavian countryside for the benefit of gruesome images of the return of the Führer in Europe.

Available crime statistics, we mentioned above, would dissuade anyone who seeks to whip up nightmarish fantasies. This is true, and positive nationalists do exaggerate. There is, then again, room for some concern about the crime level among migrants – a concern or perhaps pessimism that, worth underscoring, is not based on emotions but on data. We recently published a report: Ethnicity and Criminality – an update of the 2005 Swedish report by the Crime Prevention Agency – the first major scientific investigation into the matter in almost 20 years. In Sweden 2017, data showed 58 per cent of those suspected for crime on reasonable grounds were migrants. The corresponding figures for murder and manslaughter was 73 per cent.[9] This is important data in itself. It is also important, because one might otherwise have the impression that both sides are equally mistaken, or that a scientific analysis somehow must be "neutral" and end up in the middle. But, as already noted by Max Weber, even though a scholar is forbidden to use the lecture hall for his own

Moral show-off; self-abasement **67**

political interest, he has all the right to present any result as long as it is based on science.

As soon as our report was published, pessimists on either side raised complaints. The report was purely descriptive and based on government data, but neither pessimist took note of it. In Denmark, left-wing journalists said "suspected for crime on reasonable grounds" is a vague category, and they hurried to fill the void with Swedish "structural racism" to undermine our findings further. There is cultural self-abasement at play on many levels here. "Structural racism" is not a scientific concept but a moral one. It is used only by masochist nationalists in academia and politics to flog their own backs and announce their virtue. It corresponds to Orwell's idea of a class engaged in fictitious self-harassment while "getting a kick out of it" – looking down in horror on those who still claim a sense of self-respect. Collectivist self-loathing might seem very humble and inclusive, but the fact that you are on the cultural defence does not mean you don't have to give evidence for it. And structural racism was never supported by hard data. Also, if you question "suspected on reasonable grounds" as a good approximation of a verdict, you should support it by evidence. Otherwise, it merely looks like baseless self-criticism, as if Sweden's legal system is as unreliable as the one in Thailand.

Often, these left-wing self-accusations do not stand the test of reality, but as long as they are vague – such as repeating "well, it is actually more complicated than that," or "I am not so sure" – about the weight of "reasonable grounds," masochist nationalists might appear critical, in fact as true intellectuals. There is an entire entourage of masochist nationalists in Western academia engaged in concealing crimes among migrants, but when the suspect is Caucasian, any alarming figure is taken for granted, partly, perhaps, because those who are supposed to assess the scientific quality of it are also often smitten by cultural self-denial.

Positive nationalists, however, seemed just as discontent with our updated report above on migration and crime, and equally eager to either dismiss it, or reshape it according to their no less radical interests. The government data in the report could simply not satisfy their pessimistic view of migrants. Rape figures, we were told, must be much worse. In contrast to other trends, data on rape did not show rising figures, but slightly declining ones. These figures were the only one's taken up by the left; not because they were true (they were all true), but because they were in accordance with the views of the left. And now, incidentally, the figures on rape was the only data questioned by positive nationalists – not because they were incorrect – none of it was – but because it failed to comply with the views of the right. These are the rape data, we told positive nationalists. You say it does not show "what we want to see." But we are not interested in supporting any views. We want to see this, because it is true. The pessimism on either side was overwhelming, either to insinuate that the crime rate among native Swedes was significantly higher, or to claim crime among migrants was toned down for fear of rioting citizens.

68 Moral show-off; self-abasement

The last example of masochist nationalist pessimism I wish to bring up relates to a particular feature in any form of romantic/sentimental rhetoric – namely a tendency for ethnic stereotyping. It was above noted that positive nationalists see themselves as one homogeneous entity, and any act of violation against any one of "us" is an act against all of us. Everything is magnified and the individual is hi-jacked for collectivist objectives. The masochist version of this is that any act of violation by any one member of "us" is an act committed by all of us. These are two manifestations and one principle. In 2001, the author was interviewed for an academic position in Malmö, Sweden. The conversation with the two academics in the staff recruitment team was pleasant. Then a topic came up. In 1995 Gerard Gbeyo, a black teenager from the Ivory Coast – had been brutally murdered in Klippan – a nearby small town, and the assassins were skinheads. The two men in front of me became quiet and looked down. I sensed they were ashamed of what the skinheads had done, even though none of us, other than Swedish passport, had anything in common with those two murderers. I felt that I, too, was invited to look down in shame. But I didn't. I waited for the job interview to continue. Yes, this was a horrendous murder. But what did I, or these two men, have to do with it? I was overcome by a creeping allegation. I was a Swede, and was I not somehow complicit? But I would not have participated in the killing of Gbeyo. I might even have tried to save him. Why shouldn't I save him? Are all Swedes monsters because some skinheads are Swedes? The clockwork of masochist nationalism was under sway: We were also Swedes – ethnic co-patriots with the skinheads, and hence also guilty of the crime – and the skinheads would not be happier at the sight of this act of Aryan camaraderie. While positive nationalists never missed an opportunity to expand any wrongdoing against any native into a cause for collective, ethnic aggression against outsiders, masochist nationalists were busy doing something opposite and yet similar. They never lost a chance to multiply any wrongdoing by any native against a non-native into a source for collective, ethnic mourning and shame.

As I saw the men sitting there with their heads down, I sensed they were somehow pleased. It was as if they, as Orwell said, got "a kick" out of it. Real pain has something uncontrolled about it. But the men had leaned forward so carefully and now they were shaking their heads ever so gently, as if they had done it many times before. It was all too composed and theatrical. It was moral show-off, and I knew it. This was not real pain, but pleasure in pain; masochist nationalism on display. They toyed with compassion and collective guilt, and it made them feel righteous and elevated. They were ashamed, and it was a good and deep feeling, and an apt replacement for bygone religious submission. In their hunger for moral haughtiness they did not even shy away from exploiting a dead teenager, much like the suffering of the Jewish people has offered career-paths to cold-blooded opportunists.

In case a native European violates an individual from overseas, this is seen as an assault against an entire ethnic community, and we bow our heads in collective

Moral show-off; self-abasement **69**

disgrace. When Marwa El-Sherbini – a Muslim woman from Egypt – was killed by a German of Russian decent in Dresden in 2009, thousands of Germans burst into collective self-critical mourning. Within hours, one thug's act was coined "German Islamophobia." But was it? Wouldn't most Germans have tried to help her if they only could? If they are all smitten by structural Islamophobia, why bother about Muslims? When a non-European violates a European native, Media in the West presents a reverse scenario: this is a tragic act by one single, lonely, confused individual, against one, single, unfortunate individual who happened to be in the wrong place at the wrong time. Nobody who has a public reputation to cater for would suggest it may have cultural roots. There is no mourning, no collective allegations, and no street in far-off lands renamed in commemoration of a dead European. A few months before the assassination of El-Sherbini, a seventeen-year old French girl on holiday in Cairo was killed in a Muslim terrorist attack. On Wikipedia, El-Sherbini is covered by eleven subheadings, including notes and references. The French girl is not even mentioned. Who remembers Cécile Vannier?[10]

El-Sherbini's assassin, moreover, came from Russia. Wasn't that important? Why were Germans who would never commit such a terrible act so eager to take on the blame, telling lies about their own disgrace? Because shame is a trophy among masochist nationalists. They saw it piling up around El-Sherbini's murderer and decided to steal the indignity out of his hands.

In this discussion, I have tried to show to what extent positive and masochist nationalists are influenced by pessimism. The dynamics of pessimism within extreme, emotionally charged ideologies leads to the question: What comes on top? Nationalism or pessimism? Below it will be argued that nationalism – on behalf of any one culture of spiritual affinity – sometimes only comes second. When their nation of upbringing is either defended – or attacked – by their adversaries, our two nationalists are trading places, letting lose their despair and pessimism in the opposite direction.

In a campaign-style rally in Florida, on Saturday 18 February, 2017, President Trump alluded to a major Swedish incident the previous evening: "You look at what's happening last night in Sweden." "Sweden, who would believe this? Sweden." But no such thing had happened. A riot in the Rinkeby suburb of Stockholm a day later, however, fanned the flames of the debate, and Trump said it proved his point. Soon thereafter, Stockholm was hit by a terror attack killing five – a truck running at high speed along the pedestrian street of Drottninggatan until it came to a crashing standstill at the entrance of Åhléns – a department store. Then, American video journalist Tim Pool went to Sweden and claimed he was escorted from the Stockholm no-go suburb of Rinkeby by the police after masked men started coming after him. His film was followed by other ones, such as Pelle Neroth's Sweden – Dying to be Multicultural, where the author was interviewed. The events attracted attention by the far-right journalists Mike Cernovich and Jack Posobiec, whose film about Malmö – Invasion! How Sweden became the rape capital of the West – is a good illustration of

70 Moral show-off; self-abasement

positive nationalism in motion, i.e. a deeply pessimistic, racist picture of the city where a few innocent black men were depicted as rapists. To make things worse, the author of this book was cut and pasted into the film supposedly bringing some academic credibility to it. Cernovich and Posobiec had simply given false names, and, without further ado, added Neroth's interview with me into their own film. Not much to do about it, except lesson learned about the mind-set of a far-right winger.

In addition to the previous gloomy depictions of the Swedish countryside made by politically correct left-wingers, Sweden was once again the target of emotionally charged criticism, this time, however, by right-wingers. As a result, the tables were turned. Yesterday, no accusation against Sweden was deemed too roguish not to pass for good journalism among masochist nationalists. Under the exciting spell of trampling jackboots, anti-Swedish fantasies developed, as it seemed, into a proper academic discipline. And from the other end emerged self-haughty right-wingers piercing those dreadful left-wingers down their nose, dismissing any accusation against their beloved country as disgraceful and unfounded. Then, a reverse scenario presented itself. Now, our country was criticised by the Trumpian alt-right saying our country is under attack by migrants. Therefore, Swedish journalists, politicians, and academics – who had not made a name for themselves as patriots, were now looking down on those ungrateful right-wingers, dismissing any indecent accusation against our fine country as "undermining our international image." Self-abusing opinion, Orwell might be paraphrased, is largely a replica of jingoism in reverse colours, hence that recurring scenario, the traitor in one crisis who is a good patriot in the next.[11]

The language used by those who now, suddenly, had rediscovered their warm feelings for their home country, brought back memories of old-school nationalists. When Katerina Janouch, author and journalist originally from Czechoslovakia, in Prague made a few critical remarks in the media about Sweden's refugee crisis, Prime Minister Stefan Löfven referred to her as "a person who, in my view, makes a most remarkable statement;" and Carl Bildt, former Swedish Prime Minister, said: "clearly, Sweden has been described in a number of problematic ways."[12] The problem, then, was not Sweden, but Katerina Janouch's description of it. It is hard not to interpret these two statements as anything but an upper-class attempt to curtail dissent and criticism against the state of Sweden.

When their respective nationalism – positive or masochist – is put to the test, even nationalism itself starts to crumble. All that is left is pessimism – a dark sentiment in which their nationalism has been framed. When the situation gives the positive nationalist no other option, he will turn his pessimism towards his own nation, much like Hitler in the end wanted Germany to succumb in fire and ashes. If a masochist nationalist is forced to it, he will compromise his exoticism by starting to throw loving glances at his home country. While the core of his new-found passion for his native country might be the

Moral show-off; self-abasement **71**

same as before – namely migrants from overseas – it will all spill over to a most ordinary nationalism, hard to tell apart from any positive nationalist attitude. At the core of these frantic nationalisms, then, nationalism itself may be traded if the pessimism and darkness of their persuasion is at stake. While a positive nationalist, if pressed, is happy to have his homeland perish, a masochist nationalist would gladly defend it until the bitter end if the situation requires it. Not even their home country seems to offer a safe node of orientation – whether as subject of disapproval or admiration. When "we" are besieged by "them," our country, concludes the positive nationalist, must perish in flames. This is the self-annihilating seed inherent in any rightist discourse between Fox News and National Socialism. When "we" are accused by positive nationalists for inviting migrants to dissolve our society, argues the masochist nationalist, our country must be defended at all cost. This is the surprising streak of flag-waving lurking inside any anti-nationalist. At first glance they are saying different things. But at a closer look – or perhaps a more distant – they are very much alike.

But isn't the basic scheme presented here fundamentally misconceived? Isn't left-wing ideology, as opposed to conservative cultural despair and right-wing pessimism, at its heart constructive and optimistic? This is all very true, but one should not forget one of the most notable – and overlooked – tensions in modern politics, namely the one between the classic left endorsing progress and modernity, and the masochist nationalist left – where optimism as a political foundation – regarding technology, social progress, universalism etc. has given in to an emotionally charged pessimism, chiefly fuelled by an anti-Western attitude comprising technophobia, sectarianism, exoticism, sentimentalism and, above all, pessimism as a key outlook on the world. Today, the classic, progressive left with all its great virtues and achievements, has been side-lined by masochist nationalism which, as I have tried to show, is as sentimental, self-aggrandising, irascible, self-pitying and pessimistic, as any positive nationalist idea ever was. The one difference is that while the latter tends to whip up clouds of pessimism from the standpoint of a tormented domestic majority, the former manufactures the same sentiments from the perspective of overseas' ethnic communities. The way to overcome programmatic political pessimism – namely realism, cultural self-restraint, and a will to overcome ethnic anguish – is carefully avoided by both sides. Masochist nationalist onslaught against positive nationalist pessimism is exaggerated. The question whether we are threatened by them or they are threatened by us is not determined by political pessimism in one or other direction, but by empirical analysis. Whether we unite in rage or in shame, we unite. In terms of the sentiments, and the scope of their respective pessimism, there is little difference between positive and masochist nationalism.

While positive nationalists say we are imperilled by foreigners, masochist nationalists say migrants are endangered by neo-Nazis. The individual has left the stage. Both nationalists prefer populist simplifications to crime data. As a

72 Moral show-off; self-abasement

result of their joint self-pitying pessimism, both positive and masochist nationalists have lost the ability to respond to arguments by means of counter-arguments. Instead, they cry about being hurt, and they transform an exchange of ideas into a case for law enforcement. Their intellectual predisposition is unfit for the modern world – not surprising regarding old-school conservatives, but surprising for self-proclaimed left-wingers. When positive nationalists are overwhelmed by pessimism about their country, masochist nationalist decide to defend it with no sense of inner ambiguity.

Lack of generosity

In the previous discussion, it was claimed that we are threatened by them, or they are endangered by us. The antagonism is superficial. This leads over to another similarity. In different ways, both manifestations of nationalism lead to stinginess. Whether you praise your own country or keep belittling it, your generosity with less the fortunate people will suffer.

The reason why positive nationalists are against assisting poorer countries goes without saying. We are better than everybody else. We deserve our fortunes, and their poverty serves them right. Just look at them. So why should we open our wallet? This attitude – a sense of superiority plus a comfortable feeling of reason and logic in it – was always behind positive nationalist scantiness. But why would opponents to positive nationalism end in a similar attitude? After all, positive nationalists lack compassion, and the contrary to this, one would assume, is altruism, humbleness and generosity. Yes, this is all true, masochist nationalists are not egotists – at least not on the surface of it. But masochist nationalists, we should remember, deride their own culture with the same intensity as positive nationalists scorn cultures overseas. Therefore, masochist nationalist humbleness does not emerge out of humility regarding our luck, but regarding our misfortune. We do not hold our heads down because others' situation is more difficult than ours, but because our situation, more or less, is equally precarious. We have come to believe that bringing up our privileges is insensitive, and we are not troubled by the fact that progress, then, is ruled out for all of those who we are gazing at with such sympathy. The ambitious socialist project has been side-lined by convenient anti-racist indifference.

When we can't overcome that embarrassing barrier of class, intellectual knowledge is ruled out. In order to understand their plight, we must be on the same level as they are; i.e. share their suffering. Acknowledging our good fate no longer means they can gain access to our modernity. It means we may be labelled imperialists. We can't talk about our privileges or even admit it to ourselves, for instance that a Scandinavian earns about as much per hour as an Ethiopian lucky to have a job earns in a month. Although even masochist nationalists must recognise that countries sometimes appear different, this is mostly a cause for kitschy excitement drenched in "structural affinities," "deeper parallels," "hidden relations" and so on. We must not pass judgements

Moral show-off; self-abasement **73**

on others until we've cleaned in front of our own doorstep, and there is always the dirty corner in the room.

This attitude does not make us generous. Why should we be, when our situation is no better than anybody else's? Even though this self-depreciation may sound humble and eloquent, the net result is myopic. This is self-hatred (which may be charming to some), but it is nationalist self-obsession nevertheless – be it in reverse colours – leaving the predicament of others out of the picture.

To quote Orwell, whether we "boast" or "denigrate," we end up in the same corner. Boasting requires only lack of restraint, and an emotional, self-consumed personality. Denigrating does not take more than passion, wealth, bad conscience, and a capacity to feel pleasure in pain. While positive nationalists are self-obsessed because they are better than everybody else, masochist nationalists are self-obsessed because they are not better than anybody else. Ending up with such a distorted picture regarding our own privileged situation is not possible without masochist nationalist mental artillery – exoticism, anti-intellectualism, misconceived understanding, technophobia, primitivism and relativism, vivid imagination (to invent our misfortune), a romantic perception of suffering, lack of self-respect, and, above all, an unwillingness to acknowledge the virtues of progress. Despite its radical and modernist aura, masochist nationalism is a record of reactionary sentiments.

Caught in a discussion with the Australian writer Pamela Bone in Melbourne in 2007 about rape victims in Darfur, Germaine Greer is said to have declared: "It's very tricky. I am constantly being asked to go to Darfur to interview rape victims. I can talk to rape victims here. Why should I go to Darfur to talk to rape victims?" When Bone answered: "Because it's so much worse there," Greer asked: "Who says it is?" and added "We let down victims of rape here. We haven't got it right in our own courts."[13] Why go to Darfur? Why try to help others, when we have our own misfortune to care about? An illustration of the character this book seeks to examine, Greer was eager not to give the impression of being culturally self-righteous. Like any public left-winger, she was worried about her own reputation, more, it seems, than about hundreds of thousands of black girls in Darfur who had been killed and raped.[14] From a theoretical point of view, it would be interesting to further compare Greer's cultural self-preoccupation with that of a positive nationalist. In the eyes of the victim, however, it makes no difference whether neglect come from the left or from the right.

Another illustration of these mechanisms at work was a 2002 party congress speech by Gudrun Schyman, the then leader of the Swedish Communist Party. "Discrimination and abuse" against women, Schyman said, "look different depending on location. But," she continued, "it is the same norm, the same structure, the same pattern, which is being repeated whether in Afghanistan of the Taleban or here in Sweden."[15] I was teaching Swedish for asylum seekers at the time, and one of my students – medical doctor by

74 Moral show-off; self-abasement

training – was from Kabul. I told her about the speech and asked what she thought about it: "Has she been in Afghanistan?" "I don't know," I said. "I don't think so," she smiled.

In 2008, I spent a few weeks in Kabul and on a non-existing road we went to Bamiyan where the two gigantic Buddha statues had been blown up by Islamists in 2001. Families were sitting in holes in the mountain. A man was staring at a Swedish blonde, and the next moment I saw him pounding his forehead against a wall in a shed.

What Schyman could not avoid doing, was to recognise discrimination "looked different" from one country to another. But then she rushed to conclude the underlying structures were the same. She had the opportunity to compare Sweden unfavourably with Afghanistan, and, as a trained masochist nationalist, she took it. But what kinds of norms, exactly, were being "repeated" between Sweden and Afghanistan? Even subtle distinctions, we have been taught, should be subject to scientific scrutinising. You can claim that the role of women is the same in both places only if you deny political science altogether. In order to uphold the agenda of masochist nationalism, it seems, you need to dismiss one of the pillars of modern science – namely the importance of comparisons.

Instead of Greer's and Schyman's colonial self-indulgence, one could study World Economic Forum's "Global Gender Gap Report," where Afghanistan is not even mentioned.[16] Instead, the Forum offers special papers, such as "What does the future hold for Afghanistan?," and "This is how to get more girls into school of Afghanistan."[17] Even though these documents are written by consultants trained in neo-liberal optimism, the content is extremely bleak.

At this point, one should acknowledge that Sweden combines strong features of masochist nationalism with a relatively generous aid program. One could claim this program is the result of our refusing to make favourable comparisons to other cultures. But perhaps it is the opposite way around. Our aid programs do not exist because we pride ourselves for being humble and having our heads down, but, probably, despite all of this. At the end of the road of Greer's and Schyman's chic self-abusiveness, aid may eventually dry out coupled with tear-drenched self-obsession. Why should we bother about women in Darfur or Kabul?

In order to find a way out of this mix of self-obsession and self-denial, both forms of nationalism must be avoided. Above, it was claimed that positive nationalism is founded on "a sense of superiority plus a comfortable feeling of reason and logic." But there may be little reason behind it. I never deserved this, and positive nationalists fail to see this. They assume their privileges and other's hardship is right and just. The fact is, however, that any child born in the West is just very fortunate. God rolled the dice, and there was four times six on the table.

Masochist nationalists, on the other hand, cannot stand the thought of being privileged. Hence, they talk about "deeper structures" and "inner affiliation" between a female professor and a woman in Kabul; an ambitious case of self-deception and a left-wing attempt to tear down class divisions. This is their big mistake, because only by recognising our privilege does it make sense to share it. Unless we admit our situation is privileged and essentially the product of good fortune, we will never see any reason to spend money on people elsewhere who are worse off. If Greer and Schyman fail to differ between structural violence against women in Darfur, and violence against women in the West with no support by the wider community, the very idea of women's emancipation is in danger.

When it comes to boasting and portraying their own culture as superior, there is no end to positive nationalist inventiveness. When it comes to self-criticism and defining your own culture as inferior, there is no end to masochist nationalist imagination. Why should we teach them? They can teach us. Masochist nationalists think they are humble, but in fact, they are arrogant. Self-abuse in theory means egotism, in practice western expatriates marvel at.

Addis Ababa, the capital of Ethiopia, claiming it is so unique and different, as if any deviation from clean water, paved roads, and reasonably accountable politicians somehow must be beneficial. From the point of view of altruism, positive nationalists and masochist nationalists are pulling in the same direction. While positive nationalists ignore others because they feel superior, Schyman and Greer ignore others because they feel inferior. The difference between Darfur and Melbourne is not superficial but real. The difference between a positive and a masochist nationalist is not real but superficial.

Under the cloak, they are only two paths to the same goal: moral self-importance and a chilling indifference.

Notes

1 According to the dominating discourse within social sciences, mainstream media is right-wing. Alternative media on the net is also, however, right-wing. So where are the left-wingers?
2 Kowalsky, 1992, p. 125.
3 Ibid., p. 80.
4 Ibid., p. 109.
5 "Kölner Silvester-Angriffe: 1075 Anzeigen und 73 Verdächtige." 16 February, 2016; Silvesternacht in Köln: Offenbar viel weniger Polizisten im Einsatz als gedacht. *Süddeutsche Zeitung,* 17 March, 2016; Polizisten machen widersprüchliche Aussagen zu Kölner Silvesternacht, 18 March 2016; Einsatzleiger rechnete "nicht anssatzweise" mit Köln-Exzessen, 18 March, 2016; "Mehr als 1500 Straftaten: Die Ermittlungsergebnisse zur Kölner Silvesternacht." 6 April, 2016.
6 "BRÅ: Kvinnors Otrygghet alarmerande".
7 "Feministiskt initiative"
8 Kirfel and Oswalt, 1989, p. 16.
9 Adamson, 2020.

76 Moral show-off; self-abasement

10 Abdel-Samad, 2010, p. 99.
11 Orwell, 1945.
12 "Bildt: Det har spridits bekymmersamma bilder av Sverige", 18 January, 2017.
13 Hirsi Ali, 2010, p. 225.
14 Totten, 2006, p. 39.
15 20020118 – Gudrun Schyman: 18 January, 2002.
16 The Global Gender Gap Report 2018.
17 This is how to get more girls into school of Afghanistan. See https://www.weforum.org/agenda/2015/11/this-is-how-to-get-more-girls-into-school-in-afghanistan/

9

DEATH CULT AND THE REACTIONARY ONSLAUGHT IN WIT

The reactionary onslaught on wit

Positive nationalists are not famous for their wit. Whether they talk about their hometown, their job, culture, or world politics, humour is not their prime message. Instead, it is replaced by moralism. *One America News Network* (OANN) is a good case in point, with TV-hosts more prone towards sentimentality than wit and self-irony in particular. Why do positive nationalists often lack a sense of humour? Because they are left in earlier times before disruptive modernity, ironic post-modernity, and individualism reduced Gods and kings to perspectives, and liberalism and socialism depraved positive nationalists of any pretence of "common sense." During the rise of ideologies, Karl Mannheim noted, unconscious, omnipotent traditionalism turned into conscious conservatism on the defence.

Another reason why positive nationalists often fail to see things with a bit of light-hearted distance is because they, as already noted by Orwell in the 1940s, are obsessed with victories and defeats. Everything is pretentious, acute and up-front. Who is better – who is worse? Who is to be adored, and who should we laugh at? Irony, and self-irony above all, is impossible without putting things into perspective. Incapable of scientific detachment, they throw their stakes on one side or other, and start manufacturing majestic justifications around "their cause." If it does not exist, it will be invented. It is hard to say on what side they're on, but they will always be convinced.[1] Self-reflection is stifled and a sceptical remark is countered with emotions, ad hominem, and character assassination. The world is divided into opposite categories; triumphs and humiliations, surrender and omnipotence, intimacy and distance and filth and innocent purity. This constant urge to take sides reflects the positive nationalist's tense, war-like imagination. In this framework, everything is close and sacred, far away from laughter, in particular at your own expense.

78 Death cult; reactionary onslaught in wit

When they talk, they try to crease awe and wonder, and when they listen, everything is mystified. The real world in all is shades and considerations is unbearable to them. They are so self-assured, they do not even raise their voice, hoping it will all eventually subside into mere gestures of intimacy or animosity. At first, it might all seem warm and friendly, until you realise any humorous disbelief is impossible. Positive nationalists are ill equipped to argue for their cause because this is not their preferred means of persuasion. With a positive nationalist, the world becomes heroic, exciting and yet tediously predictable. When you drive 300 kilometres in three hours, he will nail you with his eyes and sigh "Gosh! I'll be damned!," and you are invited into his cheap self-deception about fast driving as a surreal, mystical experience. If you sense what's coming and laugh evasively, saying you only had a little edge on the pedal, he is thrown back in his bed with an amputated leg, staring at you with terrible indignation. Faced with a positive nationalist, humour, realism, and self-irony are traded for a kind of majestic folly. This is the reactionary onslaught on wit.

Throughout this discussion, masochist nationalists have ridiculed claims by positive nationalists. And clearly, they are amusing in their self-consumed austerity. Whether the topic is domestic culture, euro-centric text-books or historical kitsch, their conclusions cannot quite be taken seriously. This particular way of undermining power is not new. As noted by Christopher Caldwell, a "main weapon in the eighteenth-century Enlightenment's attacks on Christianity was ridicule."[2]

Still, this only tells us what masochist nationalists find humorous. This is part of the story, but not the whole story. In order to qualify as true defenders of wit, it is about an idea and a principle. No self-gratifying nationalism is exempt from ridicule. Otherwise masochist nationalists are merely sickened by their own culture and feel an urge to laugh at it. They are "transferred" nationalists in their overseas land of worship gazing back at their homeland with a disparaging smile. Furnished with a sentimental mind-set, they feel an itch to walk about with an audacious face, and as they can't parade up and down Champs Élysées with a bowler hat without drawing national attention, they do it overseas, knowing that no Westerner with a reputation to care about would bring it up.

What happened, for instance, when the Turkish President Recip Erdogan in March 2016 was mocked by the German comedian Jan Böhmermann for being, among other things, a "goat fucker?" Erdogan reacted like anyone who can't take a joke: he filed a lawsuit against Böhmermann. More interesting, however, was the response by the German Chancellor Angela Merkel. This entire affair happened in the middle of the refugee crisis, and partly Merkel's hands were tied. Still, she could have informed Erdogan that in Germany politicians cannot tell journalists what to say. But instead, she fanned the flames by apologising for Böhmermann's poem, complicating things even further by calling it "intentionally hurtful," as if a comedian normally has no intentions.[3] Merkel behaved much like a transferred nationalist engaged in cultural self-defeatism. A true defender

Death cult; reactionary onslaught in wit **79**

of wit not only pin-points a bombastic positive nationalist, but also detects the humour and the follies overseas. And here he was – Erdogan – very silly, and still Merkel failed to take notice of it. Instead, she turned against Böhmermann and his brave decision to rise against reactionary political oppression. Merkel was not only a transferred nationalist siding against the West and all its hard-fought freedoms, but also, seemingly, a masochist nationalist, taking pleasure in Germany being humiliated by a crude voice from the past.

Many international cases relate, however, in various ways to the Muslim Prophet Muhammad. We already mentioned Lars Vilks, whose 2007 "roundabout dog" featuring the face of Muhammad had Islamists try to kill him. In September 2006, Deutsche Oper in Berlin announced the cancellation of Mozart's Opera *Ideomeneo*, because the production's depiction of a head of Muhammad raised an "incalculable security risk." It is hard not to see the humour in it. What if, for instance, that "incalculable security risk" had been applied in the 19th century on marching workers and suffragettes? What had happened to socialism and to women's emancipation? And what if Lars Vilks, an heir of the Enlightenment, would simply one day surrender? Would that foster freedom of speech, so vital for journalists even though they seem indifferent about it?

Another famous reactionary onslaught on wit was sparked by the Danish so-called "Muhammad cartoons," In the eyes of a sarcastic critic, they had a lot to offer. Religious fanatics unfamiliar with modernity, post-modernity and subjectivism. Irascible individuals speaking freely against freedom of speech. Muslim clerics who know little about scientific detachment. Cries of vengeance. Trust in blind authority. Surrender and omnipotence. Millions of sympathisers who stopped eating Danish yoghurt. Rhetoric full of suffocating mysticism. Highway signs in the Middle East saying a Danish corporation does not like the Muhammad cartoons. An insulted dead prophet. Obsession with hierarchies. Triumph and humiliation, intimacy among believers and scorn of infidels, filth on earth and innocent purity among the virgins in heaven. A religion lost on the wrong side of Marxism and liberalism. Above all, people who cannot laugh at their own expense. All those positive nationalist follies all over again. A feast for the eyes of a Western sceptic.

But nothing happened. All of those who had a cold smile prepared for anything domestic now had their heads sunk in profound self-reflection. There were hundreds of TV-discussions, articles, and conferences about the cartoons, but not once could you spot a side-glance of disbelief. No one stood up, dismissed the whole thing with an ironic comment, and left the TV studio. Everyone was composed and concerned, and *Jyllands-Posten* where the cartoons had been published went down in history as "racist." Even dissenters said it was only a matter of freedom of speech, and that they had no reason to defend *Jyllands-Posten*, even though artistic freedom is precisely about defending art you oppose. It was all triumphs and humiliations, and no one laughed at their own expense. All those pretentious positive nationalist emotions were back again, but the reaction in the West had been upturned. Everything from old-school

80 Death cult; reactionary onslaught in wit

nationalism was being negated and, hence, repeated and copied. It was that old reactionary onslaught on wit in reverse colours. Never joke about the exotic, always mock the West.

Before we move to the next discussion, another aspect of humour in politics should be addressed. Can self-irony and self-reflection somehow prevent an aestheticization of violence?

Recently, men from Jehovah's Witnesses in the US were approached by a British journalist, who had found out they saw a good family as guided by male "leadership" – Leadership, you really mean that? she asked with a thin smile. "Yes, we do," a man explained, "but it is servant leadership, we want to serve the women, you see," and back at the BBC studio it was all frosty smiles. Jehovah's Witnesses are ridiculed by masochist nationalists not because they are religious and express an outdated relation between men and women, but because Jehovah's Witnesses has Western roots. Anything Western, says Orwell, "must be in the wrong."[4]

But what is the reason behind this negative attitude towards anything domestic? Partly, it is opportunism. On the big scale of things, Jehovah's Witnesses are civilised and self-reflective. They can be mocked because no security concerns are required. It is old schoolyard logic: avoid the bullies but feel free to ridicule the silent ones. And since they don't respond to ridicule with rage, they do not really suffer – at least that's what we are told. Lack of humour and self-irony explodes into violence, which, in turn, defines suffering. Self-reflection takes the steam out of violent retaliation, and your pain is reduced in proportion to it. Violence, in turn, is merely a reflection of a previous defamation by the West, and hence always just and appropriate. It contains its own justification and calls for our compassion. You are obliged to care for us as a result of the violence we unleash on you. In this fashion, the West is tangled up in a nightmarish web of self-accusations. If we see these unsettling fantasies from a broader political perspective, one might suggest that masochist nationalist ideology, at its cultural core, is related not only to positive nationalism, but also to the bloody aesthetics of cultural figures such as the Italian playwright Pier Paolo Pasolini and the French conservative philosopher Joseph de Maistre.

Wit, then, may acquire an important political function. If it is not applied universally against any pretentious ideology or religion and manages to penetrate that shield of self-obsession to incite some self-irony and self-reflection, violence may be justified and aestheticized and our contempt for weakness, endurance, and self-reflection will increase even further. The more pain they inflict upon us, the more they suffer and the more we should be punished. This self-playing political piano is one of the mechanisms of masochist nationalism. Contempt for those who are weak and self-reflective, and a desire to justify and aestheticize violence was always an undercurrent in more radical forms of positive nationalism. Here, you could say, these sentiments are brought to life again, this time by masochist nationalists. The aestheticization of violence is let loose in two directions – either against others, or against us.

Cult of death

During the early 20th-century, part of the nationalist right increasingly failed to be attracted by a bourgeois sense of duty. Instead, the German sociologist Kurt Lenk notes, they were caught by "heroic nihilism" – an intensely romantic morality where duty towered over everything, even death. This was characteristically formulated by Oswald Spengler in his booklet *Der Mensch und die Technik:* "It is duty to remain steadfast even for a lost cause – without hope, without rescue. To remain steadfast like the Roman soldier whose remains were found in front of a gate in Pompeii, who died because someone had forgotten to release him from duty when Vesuvius erupted: This is greatness, this means to have "spirit"."[5]

The passage is replete with political idealism. Suffering must be overcome. The soldier is a mere bolt in a majestic project where staunch discipline is required. He is proud and yet submissive, willing to sacrifice his own life rather than desert from his post. That would be decadence, and he may not survive it. There are things greater than himself and he awaits his death in calm anticipation. It is all wrapped up in a tragic-romantic cult of death as an image of purity and beauty. The framework is set by Fascist utopia – the political version of the religious heavens.

After the Second World War this all came to a standstill. National Socialism had soaked down virtually any political-romantic concept imaginable. Heroic nihilism had ended up in the garbage bin of history. "The mountain," the Austrian Political Scientist Brigitte Sob remarked, "does not call anymore," After 1945, everything associated with the image of the mountain had become politically suspect, such as sacrifice, discipline, and struggle. Any serious reference to fate, death, longing, solitude, danger, duty, submissiveness was all but impossible. The utopias and the heavens did not exist, other than as tools for the exploitation of the masses. Death was neither great nor poetic. Death was grim and death was a loss. These insights were shared not only among masochist nationalists, but among liberals, socialists, and Marxists. Gradually, however, masochist nationalists started to waver. The experiences from the war faded, and their fascination by all things exotic coupled with a fashionable self-lamentation was on the rise. Modernity and progressive ideas were increasingly linked with the U.S. and the powerful, with the superficial and the faulty; while spirituality, alternative medicine and religion were associated with communities overseas seen as exotic, poetically powerless and fascinating. The rise of postmodernism gave all of it an academic legitimacy. Among masochist nationalists, multiculturalists and romantically inclined leftists, these underlying shifts of perception also meant that death itself slowly was being reassessed. Death was no longer as horrifying as it had been. In the eyes of many, it started having a poetic and peaceful tint to it. Books where afterlife and terminal illness were cast in rosy light were piling up at the airports, such as *The Complete Cancer Diaries: One Man's Journey Into Darkness, Wonder and Hope*, or *The Cancer Whisperer – How to Let Cancer Heal*

82 Death cult; reactionary onslaught in wit

Your Life.[6] British Annabel "had terminal cancer and two years to live," but the newspaper story could make anybody envious: she left her husband, bought a flat, started dancing salsa, and turned into art. This mental transformation was aided by an increased interest in Asian culture, Buddhism and Chinese poetry with its powerful lines of submission and self-annihilation. It had all the tang of peaceful ascetic elevation, and its consumers (if not producers) were often of good faith. But it was a cult of death nevertheless. The individual was being pushed aside for the benefit of ethnic communities and religion was on the rise because cultures overseas were often religious. Spiritual, otherworldly ideas about the quest for physical extinction and life after death were no longer barred due to their association with fascism and related indigenous vices but had gained a footing among masochist nationalists because of these ideas' links to non-Western societies. At least in theory, masochist nationalists were becoming enticed by heroic nihilism. They had dissociated themselves from positive nationalist cult of death only to embrace a death cult in reverse colours.

The extent to which masochist nationalists have been defending Muslim suicide bombers is a good illustration of this left-wing temptation for the obscure overseas. What is the motivating factor behind a suicide bomber? Romantic metaphysics. Bloody determinism. Submission and utopianism. Violence turned into aesthetics. Rage beyond words. Not a shade is missing on the death cult canvas. Muslim suicide bombers are worthy followers in the Fascist pantheon. Even though masochist nationalists started out as critics of cult of death, their self-hatred coupled with an infatuation with the exotic gradually pushed them back into its field of gravitation. While nobody, they assumed, criticised fascist cult of death more intensely than they did, they had in fact come full circle. They had been betrayed by their own fury.

At home, not even innocent notions of political romanticism escape their critical attention. In case Thulesen Dahl, the leader of the social conservative Danish People's Party, advocates deference for the nation, masochist nationalists in academia may "de-codify the language" and try to push it towards right-wing utopianism and self-annihilation. But when ethnic minority groups express views saturated with death cult, masochist nationalists make a U-turn and find it all enriching, perhaps adding some lines about our Western aimless existence where we are alienated from the food by the length of the cutlery. Hence, they kill two flies in one blow. While sunbathing in anti-fascism, they can keep toying with fascist death cult without the slightest risk of being caught. It is, to quote Orwell, "a way of attaining salvation without altering one's conduct."[7] While positive nationalists defend cult of death at home, masochist nationalists do it elsewhere. Geographically, they are miles apart. But in terms of their allegiance to the idea of ecstatic self-extinction, they are saying much the same thing.

Backing heroic nihilism in the distance may also constitute a cultural death kiss, which in a roundabout way reminds of old-school colonialism where overseas' cultures always had to be kept in a state of backwardness – while we enjoy permanent political supremacy. In a situation where many overseas' cultures are struggling behind, any romantic advocating of exotic self-annihilation will brutally fix them to their destitution. Overseas cultures are doomed to prolonged struggle regardless whether we look down on them as positive nationalists do claiming their death means nothing, or, as masochist nationalists, cast them in a rosy light insisting their death signifies greatness.

Notes

1 Vaclav Havel once remarked he was always uncertain about his views and saw pros and cons on both sides. People often saw this as if he lacked conviction. In fact, he remarked, I am often rather convinced about being undecided and always seeing things from many perspectives.
2 Caldwell, 2010, p. 164.
3 Gedicht über Erdogan Merkel räumt Fehler in Böhmermann-Affäre ein, 22 April, 2016.
4 Orwell, 1945.
5 Lenk, 1994, p. 215.
6 Leavitt, 2015; 'When I was diagnosed with terminal cancer the first thing on my bucket list was to leave my husband', 13 May, 2017; Sabbage, 2016.
7 Orwell, 1945.

10

1789 AND THE GESTURES OF CONDESCENSION

Religious violence

What is behind religious violence? Is it religion itself – its holy texts and sacred traditions? Or is religion merely exploited by religiously indifferent interests? Is it only "in the name of religion?" Is anything sacred immunised against violence, while secular political ideologies never could be excused in the same fashion? There are many questions. Are only some religions inherently peaceful while other creeds are violent at heart? This final question leads over to our two manifestations of nationalism. Both of them seek to whitewash their religion of choice, claiming any violence linked to it is a distortion of its true faith, while any faith they dislike is violent by nature. On behalf of different religious, positive and masochist nationalists are making use of very similar rhetoric.

In the early morning of January 10, 2004, two people were shot in Knutby, a small town outside of Stockholm, Sweden. A man suffered severe injuries, and a young woman died. The woman who pulled the trigger were lovers with the pastor in the local Philadelphia Church. She had killed the pastor's wife, and almost killed her own husband. She was sentenced to psychiatric care, while the pastor deemed mastermind was sentenced for life. It was an act of violence from inside a Western creed, and our two nationalists lined up accordingly. Positive nationalists claimed the Church of Philadelphia was innocent. It was all unfortunate, tragic, and inexplicable. The Church had nothing to do with it.

The media, a stronghold for masochist nationalists, had a different view. The Church was a religious "sect" and the pastor a charismatic, dangerous "prophet." In the columns, the Church's members were portrayed in an ironic light as "remarkably happy," their bodies "swaying like trees in the breeze of worship."[1] Together, the lovers were "fighting against the pastor's demons, and normally these battles ended with sexual intercourse."[2] The pastor, commentators agreed, had talked about the devil, and appeared as Satan in human flesh.[3] Everything suggested the Christian faith was behind it.

If we turn to violence within foreign religions, the old conflict continues. Now, however, religion is being accused by positive nationalists while masochist nationalists has taken up their adversaries' excuses to the letter. Acts of terrorism by Muslims is a case in point. This is "all about Islam," positive nationalists maintain. They cite the Quran's most ghastly passages, while ignoring the dark pages of the Old Testament.

Masochist nationalists, then, perform a corresponding shift of opinions. "Not being divided, said the French President Francois Hollande after the attack against *Charlie Hebdo*, "means we must not paint people with a broad brush. (.) Those who committed these terrorist acts, those terrorists, those fanatics, have nothing to do with the Muslim religion."[4] After the November 2015 Paris attacks where 130 people lost their lives, Hillary Clinton twittered: "Let's be clear: Islam is not our adversary. Muslims are peaceful and tolerant people and have nothing whatsoever to do with terrorism."[5] "The terrorists," George Bush declared in the aftermath of 9/11, "are traitors to their own faith, trying, in effect, to hijack Islam itself,"[6] while Tony Blair referred to the 2005 London bombings as "an evil ideology" composed by "barbaric ideas," and a "perversion of religious faith." We shall defeat them, he continued, by "the power of argument, debate, true religious faith and true legitimate politics." It must be exposed "as the rubbish it is."[7] Islam has nothing to do with it.

If a Christian pastor studied the Bible for decades, it is likely to affect his actions. When Muslims commit violence calling out passages from the Quran, it appears hard to claim Islam is merely held hostage. Has it really, as Peter Townsend labelled his book, *Nothing to do with Islam?*[8] Would Christianity and Islam have survived if they failed to inspire their believers? Why do we deprive suicide bombers and abortion doctor killers of their final dignity of dying for a cause?

Both sides seem more interested in discrediting opponents than trying to see the bigger picture. Positive nationalists fail to see the traumas of living under a state of occupation. They say it is all about Islam. Hence, they ignore the extended family by the name of the clan, providing security when the state is weak, and these family structures we associate with Muslims only are also common among Christians living in the Middle East. It is not only about Islam. Masochist nationalists are no less unable to detect anything but that vile Christian faith which happens to be their own. Why, for instance, have so few sought to explain paedophilia within the Catholic Church as a terrible but understandable consequence of living your life without normal physical interaction? A distorted sexuality is probably the least one could expect. What has Catholicism to do with it?

If we return to Blair's clemencies for Islam above, he refers to an "evil ideology," and he insists it should be countered by "true religious faith." Violence,

86 1789 and gestures of condescension

he maintains, is "false" religion. Still, he does nothing to support these claims, and so they rest on little but Blair's rhetorical eloquence. Few would insist that "politics" by nature must be peaceful and National Socialism a political aberration, so why should not religions be assessed by the same sober attitude? And if not, what, then, is that mystical essence that separates an inherently peaceful religion from culpable politics? Any ideology – religious or secular – carries a seed of fanaticism; the humble farmer may turn *Blut und Boden*, environmentalists become primitivists wishing the death of humanity, the liberals use violence to spread democracy, and religious enthusiasts may burn and slander hoping for eternal bliss, and so on. To separate religion and politics in this fashion seems to be very difficult.

The role of religion is no less troublesome if we compare it to atheism instead of politics. Both positive and masochist nationalists would claim religion by nature is more peaceful compared to "empty" atheism in which, as Dostoevsky famously said, "everything is permitted." Others, however, would take a more left-wing approach, claiming that many religions, Islam among them, "were never confronted with the ordeal of modernity and the principles of doubt," which explains "the social, political, and economic backwardness of those religions." From this point of view, religion leads to violence. "The power of religion creates scarcity, and scarcity causes violence; hence, the weaker the influence of religion and the stronger the impact of atheist ideas." Adamson claims, "the more affluent the society and the fewer reason for violent social upheaval."[9] From this left-wing point of view, both positive and masochist nationalists are conservative.

And one can also question when Tony Blair says violence in Islam "must be exposed as the rubbish it is." Violence can and should be exposed, but preferably not as rubbish. Rubbish is not an explanation, but rather an attempt to avoid it. An explanation opens the door for theories and suggestions in a myriad of directions, but rubbish shuts the door to all of it. It becomes an isolated unfortunate event disconnected to any wider setting, any religion. It is a classic case of making use of strong emotions to cover up an absent analysis. Tony Blair illustrates a case of left-liberal populism to protect minority groups, such as overseas' religions. But the very same method is used by positive nationalists. Regarding Christian fanatics who murder abortion doctors, emotional outbursts are used, whether consciously or not, to avoid closer scrutiny. This is right-wing populism, trying to take the steam out of valid left-wing criticism and protect acts of religious crime within the majority population. We never use expressions such as "rubbish" and "foolish" about things we truly oppose. It seems like an attack but is really a defence. It is "just rubbish." Apologetically, Blair, in masochist nationalist fashion, refers to the 2005 London bombings as "rubbish," and a positive nationalist is likely to label any Christian abortion killer as "crazy" to insinuate that it was all accidental, and that there was no plot nor grouping behind, and that Christianity, above all, had "nothing to do with it."

Two branches of one romantic tree

In this discussion, I have sought to show that positive nationalism and masochist nationalism are linked together because both of them, under the surface of superficial differences, share numerous affinities. These affinities can all be traced back to one great historical-philosophical idea emanating in the aftermath of the French revolution. I am referring to the reaction to the Enlightenment by the name of the "Counter-Enlightenment." If the underpinnings of the counter-enlightenment are laid down, we shall hopefully see that these ideas not only form the ideological backbone of positive nationalism, but also of masochist nationalism.

Before outlining these underlying features, it is important to know why they appeared. As indicated by the term, the Counter-Enlightenment revolted against the Enlightenment. The Enlightenment cherished human rights – i.e. the link between the universal and the individual. It advocated reason, open debate, intellectualism, scepticism, and the virtues of aimless conversation. Within the realm of technology and practical life, it defended progress and science, while philosophically it cherished equality, commonalities, and the optimistic quest for understanding. It promoted science resting on doubt, rather than certainty based on belief. To the romantics of the early 19th-century Counter-Enlightenment, all of this had to be fought. Instead, they promoted emotions and passion, historical mysticism, organic collectivism, nationalism based on myths, cultural relativism, and, last but not least, the virtues of being unique and different. The arrogance of the individual along with the cold abstractions of universalism was pushed aside for the benefit of group cult. One of the most celebrated proponents of this early Counter-Enlightenment was the German philosopher Johann Herder. According to Herder, it was impossible to judge any society from the perspective of another society: each culture possessed a "singular, wonderful, inexplicable and ineradicable" identity, and its own "spirit," "ethos" and "atmosphere."[10]

Instead of the futile attempt to understand, he advocated a kind of aesthetic pessimism, combining triumphant vigour with the beauty of surrender. We were all caged in by our respective culture, and he abhorred" the assimilation of one culture by another."[11] Herder's rhetoric expresses, as noted by Patrick West, an "almost mystical veneration of culture for its own sake, an appeal to the aesthetic: the failure to grasp that cultures are not hermetically sealed, organic wholes, or the recognition that they contain tensions, or that they evolve and mutate."[12]

Six key ideas will now be presented. Based on a historical comparison, it will be argued that positive nationalism and masochist nationalism are two branches of one romantic tree. The philosophy of Herder constitutes a shared background of positive nationalism and masochist nationalism. An important aspect of Herder's philosophy is the notion of "belonging."[13] To be part of an ethnic group, culture, region, race, or religion is fundamentally human.

88 1789 and gestures of condescension

Crucial to positive nationalists, likewise, is the idea of being part of something greater and more majestic than yourself. You belong and commit yourself to the glorious destiny of your own group. From the other corner of the room, masochist nationalists insist that "ethnic" belonging and the fusion of "I" and "we" are vital for overseas' cultures. Lawrence Blum notes that W. E. B. Du Bois, one of the early theorists of multiculturalism, was influenced by Herder and that Du Bois' "*The Conservation of Races*" and his essentialist *The Souls of Black Folk* shows that he shared Herder's ideas about belonging and a collective "spirit" attached to a given race or ethnicity.[14] To both positive nationalists and masochist nationalists, the community is a safe haven and guiding principle, and they both oppose the liberal idea of self-determination. Two forms of culturalism result.

When confronted with foreign cultures and their influence on the German imagination, Herder invokes a drastic image: they devour our indigenous culture "like a cancer."[15] Here the concept of "ethno-pluralism" comes to mind. Often used by the French New Right (*la Nouvelle Droite*), ethno-pluralism is pluralism with barbed wire, seeing intrusion and colonisation in anything foreign. The fear is that French culture will be thinned out and that the intruder – in a seemingly innocuous phrase – will be subject to "the brutal rites of assimilation" resulting in a global wasteland of dying cultures.[16] The only cure: separation of cultures. Masochist nationalists cling to Herder's pessimism with no less determination. In their eyes, exotic cultures remain on the brink of extinction. Foreign (i.e., Western) influence, like a cancer, metastatically kills off one fragile culture after another. They offer two solutions. Either, as Charles Taylor suggests, societies must "take steps to ensure the survival of" any fragile culture prone to become extinct "through indefinite future generations."[17] Or, this colonisation may be averted by means of a complete fencing-off of their territory from the gruesome impact of Western modernity – i.e. separation of cultures. Whether the nationalist is old-school or gazing in anticipation towards the horizon, he is filled by the same romantic and collectivist rhetoric about the frail and the indigenous, and about the vile nature of foreign influence and social change.

A cultural entity described thus is often seen as "organic" – a body with a thinking head and active limbs. Herder often talks about it.[18] Similarly, no positive nationalism will gain momentum without notions of "wholeness" and organicism. The leader (or *Führer*) is gifted with vision and speaks on behalf of the downtrodden *Volk*, gradually transforming it into a mob at the mercy of his radical political ambitions. Masochist nationalism, for its part, revolves around the ethnic community seen as a collectivist and organic entity where the reluctant but honourable community leader is carried forth on the shoulders of a silent, grateful crowd. The multiculturalist Bhikhu Parekh claims that Herder, for all his loosely structured ideas and scientific flaws, surpassed both Giambattista Vico and Montesquieu "in his appreciation of the wholeness (.) of cultures."[19] While organicism is common in both camps, masochist nationalists insist that it should be praised when they use it but opposed when employed by the right. One nationalism is mirrored by the other. Save for the fact that masochist nationalists have sunk their souls into minorities in the West along with exotic communities overseas, they share with positive nationalists a longing for the primitive village of organic wholeness and unspoken concord, unspoiled by the impact of dissent and modernity.

"Awake, German nation! Do not let them ravish your Palladium!" Herder exclaims in an oft-cited passage.[20] He sees fearful storms on the horizon and tells Germans to take warning. These images – a passive *Volk* unaware of coming atrocities are part of right-winger's everyday vocabulary. If the focus is shifted to exotic cultures, masochist nationalists express the same emotionalism. These cultures are "proud" and must be on guard against Western influence. Positive nationalists and masochist nationalists are both *völkisch* – here or elsewhere. Culturalism of the right fuses with culturalism of the left.

"The savage who loves himself, his wife and his child ... and works for the good of his tribe as for his own ... is in my view," Herder maintains, "more genuine than that cultivated ghost, the ... citizen of the world," and those "superfluous cosmopolitans."[21] While the Middle Ages may have been full of "abominations, errors, absurdities," it also possessed something that has been squashed by modernity – "something solid, cohesive and majestic."[22] Here, Herder is a primitivist and anti-intellectualist. Who is authentic, decent, and hardworking? The simple man. Modern life leads to confusion and alienation. Intellectual curiosity stifles the imagination, and the cosmopolitan is useless and little more than a parasite. In the eyes of the masochist nationalist, modernity and all that comes with it have always been perceived with caution, because modernity means progress, the crushing of fragile ethnic groups, and the rule of the indigenous – presumably racist – all-white majority. As opposed to Western rational-mindedness, masochist nationalists cherish "the Other" and see its alternative forms of life – simple and introverted – as representing a tempting postmodern challenge to Western self-haughtiness. The positive nationalist, too, has plenty of reasons to embrace Herder's anti-intellectualism and primitivism. Idealising the poor and the downtrodden while attacking the elite and the bookish has a clear populist, nationalist ring. Right-wing populism and positive nationalism are replete with phrases such as "talent remains unseen," "true genius shuns worldly success," and "the most beautiful song was never written." To positive nationalists – intellectuals are elitist, rootless leftists. While the Middle Ages appeals to the masochist postmodernist due to its alleged absurdity and "jouissance," it attracts positive nationalists because of its reputed order and stability. The masochist nationalist primitivist fears the straitjacket of modernity, and the positive nationalist primitivist abhors it due to its alleged decadence.

The most important aspect of Herder's philosophy is, however, constituted by language. "Has a nation," he asks, "anything more precious than the language of

90 1789 and gestures of condescension

its fathers? In it dwells its entire world of tradition, history, religions and principles of existence; its whole heart and soul."[23] Let us not be feeble Englishmen, let us not pretend to be Spanish, let others be Spanish! "Let us be characteristic of our nation, language, scene, and let posterity decide whether or not we are classical."[24] If we lose our language, we will forget who we are: "But now! I cry yet again, my German brothers! But now! The remnants of all living folk-life … are rolling into the abyss of oblivion;" "We speak the words of strangers and they wean us from our own thoughts." These are all images that resonate with positive nationalist ideology. Language is a fixed, no-longer-evolving key to national unity, and language becomes a means to repel foreign intruders: "Germans, speak German! Spew out the Seine's ugly slime!"[25]

Ever since, this emotional outburst has caused a great stir among positive nationalists. Masochist nationalists and multiculturalists, however, are no less tempted by it. Charles Taylor, for instance, describes Herder as a "deeply innovative" thinker and "one of [the] pioneers" of "a more situated understanding of thinking," "who constantly stresses that we have to understand … language as an integral part of our life form."[26] If the masochist nationalist enthusiasm for language wavers at home, it is all the stronger on behalf of nations overseas, and their attitude remains hostile toward the intruders, i.e. imperialists, and later merely Westerners and modernisers.

Whether in terms of language, primitivism and anti-intellectualism, the dangers of foreign intrusion, organicism, or the virtues of belonging, Herder can be considered an ancestor of both classic and self-derisive nationalism. Still, the relation between Herder and these modern offspring is not seamless. In the case of positive nationalism, Fritz Stern's *The Politics of Cultural Despair* may bring some clarification. In this study, Stern traces the gradual transformation of the image of the peasant throughout 19th-century German literature, from a figure characterised by modesty and an inward-looking nature to, as the century draws to a close, a character more resembling a beast and an anti-Semite.[27] This shift reflects the dilemmas not only of discerning the true nature of Herder's thought but also, more generally, of the grey zone between essentially passive and forbearing conservatism and fascism. As a man who died in 1803, Herder fits into Stern's general time frame. When Herder describes the primitive "savage who loves himself and his family" rather than vainly embracing the entire world, the image is introverted and sentimental rather than vengeful and proto-fascist.[28] This savage – an expression that might sound ominous to some – is not contrasted with feeble liberals and socialists betraying their own *Volk* but with the discontented and restless globaliser. Herder's savage is passive rather than opposed to those who are passive; more of a Rousseauan primitive man, pristine and unspoiled, than a sociobiological carnivore. Herder's images of a simple life never catch fire.

Another difference in between Herder and our two forms of nationalism has to do with Herder's opinion about excessive nationalist pride. "To brag about one's country," Herder maintains, "is the stupidest form of boastfulness." He continues: "What is a nation? A great wild garden full of bad plants and good; vices and follies mingle with virtues and merit."[29] His sentimental mind-set, hesitant toward abrupt social change, makes him, Isaiah Berlin claims, opposed to imperialism of any kind, or as Berlin puts it, to "the crushing of one community by another, the elimination of local cultures trampled under the jackboot of some conqueror."[30] Herder insists on self-determination not only for "us" but as a principle. He sides with *l'uomo qualunque* – the man on the street – against authority, lofty intellectualism, and vain utopian aspirations. Why should the poor and the downtrodden suffer in the trenches "to satisfy the whim of a crowned madman, or the dreams bred by the fancy of a *philosophe*?"[31] Although Herder's writings resonate with holistic images, they never fuse into a nation as a beast. His theory, Berlin says, "entails no mythology."[32]

A positive nationalist shows little concern for other cultures. His compassion and interest are focused on his own nation. Herder, for his part, is adamant that "empathy" with foreign cultures is crucial. We must, he insists, try to understand them "from within."[33] Not only does this example point toward another discrepancy between Herder and classic nationalism; it also shows Herder as somewhat of an early multiculturalist. Multiculturalists, it is often claimed, go beyond merely being interested in other cultures. They show an "active interest" and seek to obtain the perspective from inside of the stranger himself.[34] This relativistic and abstract enthusiasm – characterised by calls to "cherish," "celebrate," "foster," and hail the unknown – has a lot in common with Herder's call more than two hundred years ago for sympathetic insight and seeing the world through the eyes of "the Other."

But, then, is Herder closely affiliated with multiculturalism? In the eyes of many of multiculturalism's critics, the answer is yes. Patrick West, for instance, labels Herder an early exponent of "hard multiculturalism."[35] According to this perspective, Herder is a red flag: a mythical figure casting his dark shadow over multiculturalism. On one central point, however, Herder and multiculturalism differ. It was previously claimed that Herder's theory does not entail any mythology – the collectivist ogre never gets on his feet. Groups are ultimately made up by creative, autonomous individuals, who partake in the great cultural project of *Volksgeist* – the distinctive soul of a particular people: "In the works of imagination and feeling, the entire soul of the nation reveals itself most freely."[36] Multiculturalism, on the other hand, was always silent about individuals. Focus is strictly on ethnic groups, cultures, or religions. Multicultural self-esteem and "ethnic pride" seem, moreover, conspicuously disentangled from the practical efforts of culturally creative individuals. "Ethnic pride," a cynic would say, does not come with artistic achievements but with their absence and suppression. From the vantage point of the individual, multiculturalism is not stained by Herder; Herder is rather tainted by the ruthlessly collectivist, anti-humanist implications of multiculturalism.

92 1789 and gestures of condescension

A further aspect that appears to dissociate Herder from both positive nationalism and masochist nationalism has to do with a distinctly modernist strain in his philosophy. "The Negro," says Herder, "is as much entitled to think the white man degenerate ... as the white man is to think of the Negro as a black beast." Herder's reputation for being *Germanic* and politically suspect does not hold ground, because he assigns the same rights from any given cultural point of reference. He continues: "The civilisation of man is not that of the European; it manifests itself, according to time and place, in every people."[37] There is no *Favoritenvolk*. Herder defends the idea that any member of any people has the right to express derisive views about any other people. Precisely at this crossroads is where the two brands of nationalism seem to falter. A black man is habitually dismissed as a beast by an old school nationalist. But he will not accept the black man's entitlement to express the same views about white people. A masochist nationalist, on the other hand, is more than happy to describe a white person as degenerate (including, if need be, himself) but does not allow a white person to use similar vocabulary against others. At this point, Herder stands out as a conservative and relativist, and yet a modernist and somehow also a Universalist, because he opposes a *Völkisch* mentality that would entitle some to a haughty self-privileging while denying it to others. Masochist nationalists are not tainted by Herder. Rather, their exoticist mirror-image of eurocentrism has a lot to learn from Herder's principled universalism, according to which an idea either applies for everybody or applies for nobody.

Gestures of condescension

Positive nationalists have a condescending attitude towards overseas' cultures. The pitch of their voice and the way they walk and hold their head signal: I am superior. This can be illustrated by slight shifts of behaviour. When people from the developing world are addressed by positive nationalists, they lower their voice and keep their heads held high to underscore a hierarchy. When they listen, they have to make an effort, because people from foreign cultures are basically uninteresting. What they actually say is less important: it is more of a racial thing. Positive nationalists find everything around cultures overseas primitive and dirty. They pay careful attention to their own customs, refuse to adjust when abroad, and intersperse everyday conversations with dismissive comments about life elsewhere. At home, they expect foreigners to adhere to our customs, ideally also in the privacy of their own apartments. Positive nationalists cannot wait to make self-congratulatory comparisons with other cultures. They are keen to find faults in cultures overseas and refuse to see their own historical responsibility. Positive nationalists never miss an opportunity to correct the language of others. When overseas, positive nationalists find the infrastructure medieval and the power cuts a nuisance, all due, of course, to incompetent Africans and Arabs.

When masochist nationalists engage in conversations with people from other cultures, they lower their heads and speak with a gentle, higher pitched voice, because they are keen not to be perceived as patronising. Besides, they say, we have so much to learn and so little to give. When people overseas talk, masochist nationalists cannot hide their fascination. When Mulugeta, our driver in Addis Ababa, says something most ordinary, a man on mission for the EU leans forward from the backseat: "Oh really?" I get a quick glance from Mulugeta in the driver's mirror as he turns the ignition key. This is not really about what people say. Rather, it is a racial thing. When overseas, masochist nationalists learn the local custom in no time shaking hands touching shoulders with Ethiopians like any native. They dress according to the local code, and they take pride in doing it even in the privacy of their own apartments. When at home, masochist nationalists announce we all speak English. They cannot wait to intersperse cross-cultural conversations with dismissive comments about their own culture. When the pavement in their native country shows some unevenness, the system is rotten. When the holes in the pavements in Addis Ababa are big enough for two adults and a baby carriage, they laugh: "You better watch out!" Masochist academics take note never to correct the language of foreign colleagues. Students get a headache and the university is sunbathing in anti-racism. If, at home, a masochist nationalist has an upset stomach after a lunch out, the restaurant "should be sued." If his stomach revolts abroad, he admires the fresh spices, blaming his own "weak constitution." When four people on a scooter barely escape being run down by your car in the buzzling Jakarta traffic, masochist nationalists marvel and laugh at the scene: "Somehow they make it!" When standing in a poor Ethiopian village surrounded by big fish heads in a state of decomposition, huts made of cow dung and silent children, all set next to mountains and a beautiful lake, they are not distressed by the poverty but excited by the potential.

Whether you tell starving people to clean up or find their predicament ascetic and aesthetic; whether you speak in a low-pitched voice out of sheer abusiveness or in high pitch out of misconceived humbleness, your actions and gestures have no relation to factual reality but are purely fabricated. Whether your ideology tells you to react with arrogance or fascination, you fail to notice those in front of you, who may have something to say. These two responses are merely different gestures of condescension, whether they come in the form of blunt positive nationalism or are hidden behind a mask of masochist nationalism.

Poverty in an Ethiopian village is not something else. It is not a prophecy or an unfulfilled reality, but real and complete poverty. It is the realised potential of want. The purpose of starvation is not to overcome it, but to starve. Thirty years back Marxists said "reality" was only to be found in factories and among poor people, as if more fortunate surroundings were somehow fictitious.

Today's leftists and globalisers say poverty is only latent prosperity, a mere sketch of riches yet to come. But a poor village is no more a potential wealthy

94 1789 and gestures of condescension

suburb than a new Mercedes is a potential wreck. Masochist nationalists see the potential in an Ethiopian village, while early 20th-century imperialists daydreamed about the prospects in Burma, and it is hard to tell one from the other.

Another area of condescending gestures relates to how these two nationalists react to a delicate issue – namely lack of hygiene. In his preface to *The Road to Wigan Pier*, Victor Gollancz, Orwell's editor who had commissioned the writing of the book, referred to it as "a classic minor document of English middle-class left-wing intellectualism and a striking example of much Orwell was attacking." Yet, Richard Hoggart writes in the 2001 edition of the book, Gollancz "tut-tuts nervously when Orwell says that working-class people are believed by middle-class people to smell." The editor "would have been less shocked if Orwell had said that the Hampstead intelligentsia smell."[38] There are some things you can't say, even though they are true, and there are other things you should feel free to say, even though they are not true. "Of course, as a whole," Orwell admits, the workers "are dirtier than the upper classes," but since "less than half the houses in England have bathrooms," workers "are bound to be, considering the circumstances in which they live."[39]

If we turn from yesterday's workers to destitute individuals overseas, it appears as if the underlying pattern of middle-class reactions to poverty basically remains the same. At a recent dinner with people working for the United Nations, the conversation drifted towards India, where the poor at times are eating with their right hand while wiping their bum with the left hand, and cleaning it with soil, ash, or sand: "You know, you can feel the food, and you can never do that with cutlery, can you?" the hostess explained. "Oh my god, we miss that! But then, well, you know – haha! – make sure you shake their right hand because they, you know – haha! – with their left hand – haha!" Her reaction was similar to Gollancz' above. The lower classes struggle to keep clean appears to make middle-class intellectuals uneasy. Why? As such, dirtiness is trivial. As Orwell said, anyone in the same situation is bound to be dirty. Any educated person knows about the impact of social circumstances.

Still, eating with your hands is a poor option. Cutlery keeps your body clean and prevents infections. And going to the toilet with your left fingers without access to water is nothing to laugh evasively about. It is a terrible thing, and no human being should be forced to endure it. But this is maybe where things get complicated. If you pay attention to the reaction among those who try to avoid the topic of others' lack of hygiene, you'll notice there is often something unforgiving about it, or at least that has been my impression after socialising with UN expatriates for more than a decade. They do not laugh out of consideration, but, as it appears, out of distaste because they are not quite convinced someone who goes to the toilet with his left hand is fully human.

How is this possible? What happened to the left and their sympathy for the downtrodden? Perhaps the reason, as I have already touched upon, has to do with

1789 and gestures of condescension 95

that multicultural assumption that the only appropriate way to approach other's deprivation is to deny it altogether, because unless you do, your own privileges will be obvious, which is culturally insensitive and "racist." The recognition of worker's dirt, they would tell you with a stern look, would "play into the hands of" those who oppose workers. The entire socialist tradition of economic development and social change has been handed over to the far right on a silver plate. And if you keep denying others' hardship out of middle-class humanitarian misapprehensions, those radical insights will eventually start wearing off. One day, you will no longer see a poor Indian man among his utensils enslaved by lack of options. You will see an animal.

On the face of it, this masochist nationalist attitude towards dirtiness among the downtrodden is very different from how a positive nationalist might react. But from the point of view of a person with no access to soap and water, there is little difference. Whether you callously point fingers at other's struggle to keep clean, or laugh evasively about it, we're merely witnessing two forms of condescending gestures at dirtiness among the poor. In either case, social improvement is stifled, and the poor may be caught forever in their destitution. Clearly, there is a danger of pointing out other's dirtiness. You know you are clean and they are not, which may bring out political demons. But there is also, in a more round-about way, a danger of evading other's failure to keep clean, because, after all, it is not a choice but the lack of it. If these individuals exercised their freedom, they would *not* be dirty. "It is," Orwell maintains, "a pity that those who idealise the working class so often think it necessary to praise every working-class characteristic and therefore to pretend that dirtiness is somehow meritorious in itself," and "healthy and 'natural,' and cleanliness (.) a mere fad or at best a luxury." The sentence strikes a note that carries though the entire second section of Orwell's *The Road to Wigan Pier*, namely the extent to which the upper class left fails to understand working class reality. "They seem not to see," Orwell continues, "that they are merely giving colour to the notion that working-class people are dirty from choice and not from necessity."[40] To the left-wing middle-class, with limited experience of dirt outside of horse stables and the artist's studio, chaos, damp, and unpainted walls send signals of creativity, dissent and frivolous sexuality. The walls of the truly destitute, however, are not in "earth colours" – they lack paint. By casting lower classes' dirtiness in a rosy light, left-wing academics find a way out of their bad conscience. Even more important, perhaps, is to maintain the illusion of dirt as a choice, accomplishment and quest for purism. If the lower classes would come out as an aspiring bourgeoisie only deprived of material well-being, the middle-class patrons, in turn, would be deprived of their moral beacon and victim of middle-class abuse in one – namely the lower classes. If they would welcome running water and a bottle of perfume, the entire left-wing edifice would come tumbling down. Hence, the middle-class left has all the reason to retain the lower classes in an everlasting state of uncleanliness to be

96 1789 and gestures of condescension

admired – or secretly despised – from afar. After all, while she praised eating with your fingers above, the hostess still kept using her Sunday cutlery.

It is not difficult to replace Orwell's middle-class intellectuals and their vain ideas about worker's dirt as choice with today's exotifying masochist nationalists hoping that shortage of water and soap overseas is in fact an achievement. It is basically the same lofty idealism among the left-wing middle classes. And this masochist nationalist attitude, in turn, is not unlike that of a positive nationalist. Masochist nationalists seem to have little interest in improving sanitary conditions among the poor, and positive nationalists – at least those further to the right – also care very little about it. While the latter claims the poor chose their dirtiness – which serves them right, the former also suggests it is based on free will, which, in contrast, makes it so alluring and admirable. In this sense, both of them dismiss the stifling impact of social conditions. If the poor had a choice, they would manage to keep clean. While masochist nationalists want to preserve dirt, damp and chaos overseas because they are enamoured by it, positive nationalists, as in a mirror image, wish to retain it in far-off lands because they so strongly oppose it. Finally, they are both shocked at the sight of the poor's struggle to keep clean. Positive nationalists are abhorred by lack of hygiene among certain overseas cultures and blame the individuals for it, while masochist nationalists refuse to accept the destiny of poverty, which sends them into a middle-class spiral of envy and revulsion. These are, on the surface of it, very different and perhaps even opposite gestures, but they both, nevertheless, express a genuinely condescending attitude towards the destitute, whether at home or overseas, and their attempt to preserve human dignity under difficult circumstances.

As a final case of condescending attitudes, we will touch upon the illusions of distance – and intimacy – respectively. Illusions of distance emerge among positive nationalists. Faced with individuals from afar, a positive nationalist wants to tell everybody just how alien and impenetrable he finds them. He would never make any attempt to socialise, and he'd be appalled in case he would be forced into some kind of proximity to an outsider – a new Turkish neighbour or a black son-in-law. Even the slightest difference in habit is magnified into an abyss. Above all, he defends cultural distinctions to the extent they appear almost tangible. Against these illusions of distance stands, however, masochist nationalist illusions of intimacy. An overseas' family next door would make him remarkably excited and he would not lose a minute to break "cultural prejudices," as he calls it. In the eyes of a masochist nationalist, it is all about "humanity," and not even significant cultural differences would dissuade him from constantly trying to get personal. The very term "cultural prejudices," he might happily tell you, rests on the assumption that any disagreement or failure to communicate is based on misunderstandings or lack of information. If we only talk things through, we will all agree.

Clearly, while it is dangerous to erect walls between groups of people, it is no less dangerous to suggest they are entirely fictitious. From his perspective

1789 and gestures of condescension **97**

in the 1940s, George Orwell mainly talks about class differences, but you may easily apply his analysis on today's masochist nationalists and their efforts to cross cultural divides:

> Hence the eager class-breaking activities which one can see in progress on all sides. Everywhere there are people of good will who quite honestly believe that they are working for the over-throw of class-distinctions. The middle-class Socialist enthuses over the proletariat and runs "summer schools" where the proletarian and the repentant bourgeois are supposed to fall upon one another's necks and be brothers for ever; and the bourgeois visitors come away saying how wonderful and inspiring it has all been (the proletarian ones come away saying something different.)[41]

Positive nationalist illusions of distance, as it seems, are taken to its opposite extreme. Class divides means nothing, and no activity is more praiseworthy and supposedly successful than suddenly getting intimate with those on the opposite end of the social staircase. Orwell notes in brackets, however, workers' reactions to these "wonderful" moments of class-breaking activities. Their feelings, Orwell suggests, is not inspired at all, but rather hostile – a sense of being pawns moved about on some inexplicable moral board-game. At this point, then, hypocritical illusions of intimacy merge with vicious illusions of distance. Whether you hide behind walls of class of culture, or pretend as if your privileges are worth nothing, they will see through it, and in both cases hostility will keep mounting. Here, we need to return to the hostess above praising eating with your hands, even though she does not do it herself. Many people, Orwell notes, "imagine that they can abolish class-distinctions without making any uncomfortable change in their own habits and 'ideology'." This inconsistency – if you love us, why don't you live the way we do? – is perhaps one of the reasons why those illusions of intimacy will always fail.

Regarding those middle-class illusions of intimacy, Orwell makes an important distinction between outright disapproval and mere matter-of-fact difference: "However much you like them, however interesting you find their conversation, there is always," Orwell continues, "that accursed itch of class-difference, like the pea under the princess' mattress. It is not a question of dislike or distaste, only of *difference*, but it is enough to make real intimacy impossible." Moreover this "class-breaking business" may go horribly wrong. When the proletarian and the bourgeois "do succeed in meeting, (this) is not always the embrace of long-lost brothers; too often it is the clash of alien cultures which can only meet in war."[42]

Stop calling me "sir," you chaps. Surely we're all men? Let's pal up and get our shoulders to the wheel and remember that we're all equal, and what the devil does it matter if I know what kind of ties to wear and you don't, and that I drink my soup comparatively quietly and you drink yours with the noise of

98 1789 and gestures of condescension

water going down a waste-pipe – and so on and so on and so on; all of it the most pernicious rubbish, but quite alluring when it is suitably expressed."[43]

The conflict is described as rather violent, but Orwell does not in the least support some pessimistic, far-right antagonism. His sole concern is the lack of honesty among middle-class left-wingers. Change has to come, but only in due course: "If you think of yourself as a gentleman and as such the superior of the greengrocer's errands boy, it is far better to say so than to tell lies about it. Ultimately you have got to drop your snobbishness, but it is fatal to pretend to drop it before you are really ready to do so."[44] In this sense, you could say that George Orwell stands firmly between our two nationalists – sober enough not to buy into any whimsy ideas about forced intimacy, and yet clear about the fact that one day those privileges of culture and class will have to go.

Notes

1 Tät gemenskap både välsignelse och förbannelse, 21 January, 2004.
2 Wikipedia: Sara Svensson.
3 Tät gemenskap både välsignelse och förbannelse, 21 January, 2004.
4 Statements by François Hollande, 2015.
5 Hillary Clinton on Twitter, 2015.
6 Text: President Bush Addresses the Nation, 20 September, 2001.
7 Kumar, 2006, pp. 3-6.
8 Townsend, 2016.
9 Adamson, 2011, pp. 83-87.
10 Parekh, 2000, p. 68.
11 Ibid., p. 68.
12 West, 2005, p. 12.
13 Herder, 1877-1913, p. 8:210; cf. 8:303.
14 Blum, Lawrence, I'm Not a Racist,... But -The Moral Quandary of Race (Ithaca, NY: Cornell UP, 2002). (Blum hade fallit bort. Vad gäller "Du Bois" XX and XY, står det under "Bois".
15 Herder, 1877-1913, p. 25:11.
16 Wolin, 1998, p. 54.
17 Malik, "Making a Difference: Culture, race and social policy", pp. 361-78.
18 Berlin, 1998, p. 416.
19 Parekh, 2000, p. 67.
20 Herder, 1877-1913, p. 17:309.
21 Ibid., p. 13:339.
22 Ibid., p. 5:527, 524.
23 Ibid., p. 17:58.
24 Ibid., p. 2:57.
25 Ibid., p. 17:129.
26 Taylor, 1997, pp. 79, 91.
27 Stern, 1974.
28 Herder, 1877-1913, p. 13:339.
29 Ibid., p. 17:211.
30 Berlin, 1998, p. 373.
31 Ibid., p. 373.
32 Ibid., p. 416.

33 Herder, 1877–1913, p. 10:14.
34 Eriksen and Stjernfelt, 2008, p. 344.
35 West, 2005, pp. 8, 10.
36 Herder, 1877–1913, p. 18:58.
37 Ibid., p. 18:248–49.
38 Orwell, 2001, p. vi.
39 Ibid., p. 121.
40 Ibid.
41 Ibid., p. 150.
42 Ibid., p. 154.
43 Ibid., p. 149.
44 Ibid., p. 156.

11

RACISM

In this discussion, I have tried to show similarities between two forms of nationalism. Both of them treasure their own culture of spiritual identification along with its roots and biased textbooks. They are both enticed by kitschy, misty origins whether here or overseas. They share an obsession with past injustice and idealise homogeneous groups and the difference between them is underscored. Laws and customs from their culture of preference may be imposed on cultures they deem inferior. Positive nationalists overlook minority oppression and masochist nationalists turn a blind eye to discrimination against the majority. They are political pessimists, whether the threat comes from outside or from within.

While majestic poetry is brutalised by positive nationalists, masochist nationalists commit an opposite fallacy by confusing intellectualism with fascism. Positive nationalists unite in vengeance – masochist nationalists in shame. Positive nationalists are stingy because they feel superior, and masochist nationalists are ungenerous as a result of self-pitying narcissism. They are both equally squeamish and easily insulted, using any sarcasm as a pretext for massive retaliation. While positive nationalists say Christianity is innately peaceful, masochist nationalists insist Islam is inherently peaceful. Both nationalisms emanate from early 19th-century Counter-Enlightenment. They both have a condescending body language and attitude towards lack of hygiene.

These themes have one aspect in common. Whether you talk to people from overseas in a coarse voice or as if you are speaking down in a baby carriage, they coalesce in a sense of superiority on the part of your own culture. In one form or other they express a racist attitude. Therefore, the comparison between these two nationalisms will end with a few examples of the ways in which a racist attitude – in either direction – is being expressed in both camps.

First, both positive and masochist nationalism rest on racial hierarchies. Skin colour plays a crucial role to both of them.

Third, they are both drawn towards the pseudo-science of physiognomy.
Four, they share an obsession by the colourful.
One type of racial segregation is mirrored by another.
Six, racist name-calling is common in both camps.
They both lapse into political exaggerations.
Eight, both forms of nationalism give way to ideological stereotyping.
Nine, they both embrace the icy worldview of global capital.

Racism along the lines of positive nationalism, it will be argued, can only be countered by criticising all those ideas, generalizations and assumptions upon which racism ultimately rests – such as political stereotyping, segregation, hierarchies and physiognomy – for the benefit of solidarity and the deconstruction of ethnic walls, the rights of the individual, and critical thinking. This is about principles, not about activism. If all those dark political ideas are merely attacked in the West but supported on behalf of non-Western cultures, the West will crumble while this dark political romanticism will spread across the globe. If the positive nationalist mind-set is to be overcome, its underpinnings must be dismantled as ideas. In their passionate attacks against racism within positive nationalism, however, masochist nationalists have failed. They have merely replaced the racism of the brute with the racism of the gentle patron.

Racial hierarchies

Positive nationalists never made a secret of their hierarchical worldview. The white race is superior. The black race occupies the lowest rung. Positive nationalists find any group of black people intellectually stale, suggesting it ought to be infused by other races and the whiter the better. Positive nationalists won't generalise about whites because we are all individuals, while other races, and blacks in particular, are subject to sweeping judgments because their individuality is "underdeveloped." Black people generally lack power so why not lump them all together? This is not racism because if they were successful they would come out as individuals.

But the idea that any race is "higher" than another is outdated essentialism, we are told by Western academics with a soft spot for overseas' cultures. As individuals, they remind us, we are formed by the environment. Had I grown up in Turkey, I'd spoken Turkish. The entire collectivist verbiage is mere right-wing ideology. Still, in their criticism against racial hierarchy positive nationalist style, masochist nationalists come full circle, and merely present a racial edifice standing on its head. Any nationalist whether self-eulogising or self-depreciating, Orwell maintains, is obsessed with hierarchies.

A Danish former colleague who made an academic career out of belittling Denmark once supervised two female exchange students. When he heard that one of them was from Germany, he paused and smiled: "Well, then you can be in charge." Apparently, racist slurs against Germans are risk-free. The tables are upturned. If you generalise about black people, Yehudi O. Webster notes, you

102 Racism

may "be called a racist." Suggesting Europeans are racist is not, however, deemed racism, but a joyful grab-yourself-by-the-throat, likely to break the ice at the dinner table on Stockholm's media-savvy inner city inlands.[1] This reminds me of the self-lamentation by the academics in my job interview above where all Swedes were dragged down into an accomplice for the murder of Gerard Gbeyo. Black lives matter is now accusing the medical NGO Médecins Sans Frontières for being "structurally racist," and the allegations against "whites" as one bloc is seemingly endless. The delicate question whether medical doctors from Asia and the West might be better qualified is carefully left out of the hands-down article in the *Guardian*.[2] The lack of self-restraint among certain black politicians and activists is disheartening. What is more worrying, the organization seems to have no means of self-defence, in case it is indeed based on meritocracy. Not long ago, nepotism and sectarianism was slowly defeated by the law of merit. In case this law now is being shouted down by partial interests, the modern world is in danger.

And what about environmental concerns? The same pattern repeats itself. From the heights of their smugness, positive nationalists look down on Shanghai and New Delhi, and forget that our cities were once also very polluted. Masochist nationalists, then, turn the scheme upside down. In *Aftonbladet*, Sweden's largest newspaper, a message read: Why should Sweden, "one of the dirtiest countries in the world, invest more money in cars?"[3] This is not true but appealing to like-minded, and on arrival at Bole International Airport in Addis Ababa they eagerly inhale the cancerous scent of burnt wood, while any Ethiopian who can afford it is on her way out.

It is no longer allowed to place blacks or Muslims on the lowest rung. Instead, whites are filling the void – and happily, too, because we are on both sides of the joke. A tourist leaflet by the German city of Köln said: "All whites are racists."[4] In 2020, fanatic advocates of Black Lives Matter are shouting the same thing. There is no escape. The forgiving "environment" has given way to the verdict of essentialism. Normally, it is not accepted to say actions are caused by essentialist qualities, but if we talk about Caucasians, it is not only accepted but required. Make sure not to use is against others, but feel free to use it against us. We are racists because we are innately disgraceful.

But if self-idealization is a lie, so is self-hatred. If all whites are racists, who wrote that message? Why bother about strangers? By nature of political logic, masochist nationalist gloomy self-perception is likely to bring out unpleasant admirers, namely right-wing radicals. If we are all racists, as I wondered during my job interview above at Malmö University College, why, then, argue against racism and in favour of some kind of scientific level-headedness, as I believe I am doing here? Why not instead humbly admit defeat, and act as we are expected to: vote nationalist and start attacking migrants and journalists? This is probably the deepest riddle in this entire self-abusive approach where the racial ladder is upturned: in case there is no hope, if we are beyond rescue, why bother about inferior races? If you keep announcing to the entire world just how politically depraved you are, your sense of decency will eventually erode, and your personality may start caving in. In the end, any self-blackening humanist will, at least if he is honest and thorough about it, turn into a fascist. Similarly, there is certainly something civilised or at least comforting in a persistent denial of having a ruthless character, even, perhaps, a trifle of humanity in arrogance, because if you are hammering your virtues in public, claiming you are civilised and not a racist this may, in fact, prevent you from becoming one. We must tread carefully with the notion of humility.

But in fact, we have just touched upon another hidden similarity between positive nationalism and masochist nationalism. Whereas the latter appears to overlook the political dangers of humanistic self-depreciation – say you are a fascist and you may become one – the political dangers of the former are much more straightforward. If you walk about praising you glory, fascism is always an opportunity.

Positive and masochist nationalist agree on this: We are racists. From their opposite corners, they are both even fascists, one because of proud inhumanity, the other as a result of humanity and an exciting sense of guilt. But why claim you are a racist in the first place? In the twilight of multiculturalism, things are not quite what they seem. If you don't like communism, people normally know you are not a communist. If you don't like racism, why not say you are not a racist? If you despise something from the bottom of your heart, how come your heart is full of it? How is this even possible? Perhaps because of a twisted humanity and humbleness where your rampant self-depreciation (instead of flaming self-appreciation) turns you into a fascist.

Racial preferences are clearly expressed when it comes to our human origins. Positive nationalist insist human race was originally white, and all progress was basically because of the efforts of the white man. Other races are mere deviations of the white race; a watering down of the crystallising intensity of the occident. In order not to deteriorate, the white man should avoid contact with lower races. The murky qualities of these ideas are easily revealed: Our ancestry cannot be taken hostage for ethnic prestige in either direction. Whether our "first" ancestors were "white," "black" or of any other skin complexion is an academic question, of little interest other than out of pure scientific curiosity. Whatever our origin may be, it is interesting because it increases our knowledge. Nothing is at stake but ignorance. Any final claim does not, moreover, stand the test of relativism. There is no agreement about the precise origins of the human race. Whether we were initially carnivores or vegetarians is hard to say.

As we turn to overseas' cultures, however, masochist nationalists are suddenly uninterested in all those academic virtues. Relativism is gone. Ideas of "origin" are no longer right-wing propaganda but scientific. The idea of racial equality is gone and knowledge is in the service of ideology. "The Human species," masochist nationalists argue, "was originally black; it radiated from Africa to all other parts of the world, and it now comprises different but biologically equal racial groups."[5] The anthropologist Cheikh Anta Diop has sought to demonstrate that

104 Racism

various races correspond to civilizational achievements. His conclusions are a mirror image of positive nationalist myth-making. Suddenly, that edifice of racial pre-eminence is back on its feet, or rather on its head. The black race occupies the top rung, in a supreme position of racial hierarchies. Old-school anthropology "is upturned."[6] Master and slave have traded places, and yet little has happened from the point of view of racial hierarchies.

Skin colour

"All whites are racists," the tourist leaflet announced above. This leads over to an emblematic aspect of racism – skin colour. As we shall see, our two exponents of nationalism both embrace it, and the outcome is radical either way. The Swedish approach towards discriminatory behaviour is succinctly formalised in the Law against Discrimination (Diskrimineringslagen). In it, "skin colour" plays an important role. This is not surprising, because skin colour was always a classic racist category common among positive nationalists. However, one would expect the law to replace the sweepingly collectivist "skin" as basis for identification with our intellectual faculties that set us apart from the animals. The findings in the Law against Discrimination, however, tell another story. In § 5.3, Section 1, one of the grounds for "Ethnic belonging" is – precisely – "skin colour."[7] Your ethnic belonging, or grounds for exclusion, may be based on your skin complexion.

Why, then, reject a racist category with one hand and endorse it with another? Why say skin colour is fascist, and then suddenly announce it may define your identity? Because masochist nationalists are convinced that the pre-eminence of positive nationalist skin complexion cannot be tackled the liberal way by disputing its underlying extreme assumptions. The ground-breaking content of the liberal vindication is betrayed by the fact that it is conducted calmly, with precision which, in the eyes of left-wing enthusiasts, is seen as appalling intellectualism and almost a sell-out. Instead, masochist nationalists perform their habitual rites. With great determination they strike against positive nationalist skin colour at the price of keeping the fascist underlying structure untouched. The entire endeavour is hollow and aimless but saved by the fact that it is conducted as a tour-de-force.

The Law against Discrimination claims to work against discrimination based on colour of the skin. But it only works against white colour as a line of demarcation. If a native European would claim to be defined by his white skin, his career would come to an end. But an Ethiopian guarding the gates of the state may welcome or turn back anyone based on whether skin colour is properly Ethiopian or not. While we salute their bold determination to organise along the colour line, we make sure not to do it ourselves. The Law against Discrimination has good intentions. The problem is only that few of us, and fascists least of all, have anything but good intentions.

While claiming to oppose skin colour as a political category in theory, masochist nationalists only oppose it as a tool of their adversaries but endorse it as a weapon on behalf of their own exotic culture of choice – without any sense of inner contradiction. There is no way out of it. "References to human beings as white people and black people are," Yehudi O. Webster claims, "part of an intellectual tradition of anatomical reductionism and differentiation; they belong to the blunders of a bygone biology." It is all an "outdated anthropology" whether your elevate light skin or leather-tanned skin into a proper means of ethnic classification.[8] In the academic discussion on ethnicity and nationalism, moreover, skin complexion is virtually unknown. Neither the modernists – Benedict Andersson and Ernest Gellner – nor for that matter Anthony Smith – sometimes labelled "primordialist" – refer to skin colour or biology. Even though Smith talks about "ethnic cores" he is never referring to biology but to culture and a shared world of symbolic expressions. Not even Josef Stalin ever made use of skin colour and biology. The only ones who have defended ethnic belonging in terms of skin colour are the National Socialists, which does not support masochist nationalist's progressive self-image. Rather, it illustrates our recurring idea: masochist nationalism is merely an overseas political replica of positive nationalism.

Physiognomy

Some call it phrenology, but physiognomy is probably a more accurate expression. It is about distinguishing between human beings and races by facial features such as shape of jawbone and forehead. In mid-19th-century, Cesare Lombroso popularised it as a strand of criminology. It is ideology covered with a thin layer of pseudoscience and it suited the political ambitions of positive nationalists, just like skin colour above. Its purpose it to justify dominance of one race – often the white race – and subordination of all other races.

Historically, the convenient, self-eulogising rhetoric of physiognomy has been in the hands of old-school nationalists. As it happened, their own facial composition was elevated into role model – high, thoughtful forehead, straight, energetic nose, medium-sized jaw, and thin lips.

By analysing facial features, Lombroso claimed, you could pick a criminal. In his 1876 *Criminal Man*, Lombroso maintained he could be recognised by "enormous jaws" (.) and other features "found in criminals, savages and apes (.)" These features, he continued, corresponded to a "love of orgies and the irresistible craving for evil for its own sake, the desire not only to extinguish life in the victim, but to mutilate the corpse, tear its flesh, and drink its blood."[9] Apparently, certain facial features led to very precise expectations. But Lombroso's theories are not only targeting criminals, but black people: "the projection of the lower part of the face and jaws (.) found in negroes and animals (.): all these characteristics pointed to one conclusion, the atavistic origin of the criminal."[10]

106 Racism

It shouldn't require much more than these few distressing examples to turn your back to Lombroso's physiognomy and "scientific racism" no matter where you might find it. Attention to facial features, after all, is a classic racist attempt to deprive a person of his rights as an individual. There is no such thing as "good" physiognomy. "All nationalist distinctions – all claims to be better than somebody else because you have a different-shaped skull or speak a different dialect – are," George Orwell maintains, "entirely spurious, but they are important so long as people believe in them."[11]

And yet, a familiar political tragedy unfolds. "The racial inventory" used by certain critics of white supremacy, Webster notes, merely "reproduces the same arbitrariness that characterises earlier attempts at racial classifications," and some of their "remarks rival" those of Lombroso "in their fixation on parts of the human anatomy and on race-mixing."[12] Masochist nationalist "fixation" on the human anatomy is identical to old-school positive nationalist corresponding obsession. We are witnessing two manifestations of the pseudo-science of physiognomy.

One difference in between them should however be pointed out. While physiognomy, in the hands of positive nationalists, is a stigma to be put on those who are inferior, masochist nationalists try their best to fuse physiognomy with superior qualities of charm and attraction. A good example was found in the tourist leaflet from Köln above. "We love," the editorial declared, "human beings with different skin colour and shapes of their head."[13] This is one among many similar cases. What is more, this example is only an explicit formulation of something very familiar since the early days of global travel, namely the exotifying sentiments of a certain breed of left-leaning white intellectuals about bodies and faces of overseas' races and the black race above all. To make bad things worse, given the fact that bringing up someone's facial composition as a judgment of character is an insult and always will be, it would be fair to say that the positive nationalist at least should be given credit for his brutal honesty, while the masochist nationalist veers off into a psychological quagmire, namely to try to turn a political abuse into a compliment.

This is not really about physiognomy. This is about whether you are on the right side or the wrong side. All that's left at the core of masochist nationalist tolerance is a power game. If you are on the wrong side – i.e. if you believe classic nationalism – if modest – can be a good thing, and, if pressed, express mild appreciation about your country's achievements, little is allowed. Everything will be held against you. But if you are on the right side, you can be much more vulgar, silly, poisonous and dishonest – than you would ever dare to be on behalf of your native country. With the credulity of a child, you can use obsolete and colonialist labels and support facial features that would rival any National Socialist. This is old school imperialism in reverse replay. The European face is racist. The oriental face means emancipation. In the end, if you distil it, only the fist remains.

If you wish to oppose positive nationalist fixation with physiognomy, you must oppose the entire scheme of physiognomy irrespective of who might profit

Racism **107**

from it, and who might be endangered by it. If you merely attack it in the West while embracing exotic head shapes, you are fuelling overseas' cultures with a lazy and dangerous ethnic justification. You are also merely replicating and reinforcing the pseudo-scientific racism of physiognomy.

Obsession by the colourful

Another example of this flair for the visual is to call a society "colourful." It is common among both types of nationalist. In English, masochist nationalists label it as a "colourful community." In Norway this translates into "fargerik felleskap." Whenever immigrants were mentioned on Norwegian TV or in the press, Bruce Bawer notes, "you could be sure these words would figure prominently. Norwegian journalists, professors and politicians loved to use the term."[14] In Sweden we say "mångfald" (diversity) or "regnbågssamhälle" (rainbow society) – suggesting an open society where every colour of the political palette is "represented" and "celebrated." Still, this approach only mirrors positive nationalism. Starting out from old-school imperialism's exoticism and racist excitement for the colourful, optic imagery of clans and tribes – be it baskets of spices or civil war – masochist nationalists have come full circle, proudly announcing their fascination for all things exotic, declaring their remote culture of esteem as a whirl-wind of flamboyant traditions. Other, more troublesome aspects of exotic cultures such as civil war or Female Genital Mutilation (FGM) are sometimes ignored by positive nationalists because they are not interested in it, while the same dark traits are sidestepped by masochist nationalists because it would taint their idyllic image and also, they keep reminding themselves in horror, play into the hands of a party back home in Europe they chose to label "fascist." In both cases, it fits the mind-set of an arrogant and possibly racist bourgeoisie.

Bruce Bawer notes that this "fixation on skin colour mocked Martin Luther King's dream of a colour blind society, and its reduction of immigrants to their most superficial aspect turned them into mere window dressing – an outward sign of ethnic Norwegians' inner virtue."[15] King's famous dictum says a lot about what is going on. On the one hand we have the great Martin Luther King, enlightened leftists and Marxists, feminists un-crippled by relativism, cautious universalists, liberals who take this label seriously – who all say colour does not count; and on the other hand an unholy alliance of positive nationalists and masochist nationalists – multiculturalists, adherents of political correctness, self-abusive liberals, imperialists, old-school racists, fascists, radical conservatives, Islamists, relativist feminists and political enthusiasts who all insist colour does count. A French pro-verb – Les Extreme se touché (the extremes meet) – catches the essence of this. Positive nationalist and masochist nationalist adulation of the colourful belong to the same basket of ideas. If only they knew how much they had in common. When two ends of a rope are put together, previous extremes are combined. On one end sit colour-obsessed self-lovers and

108 Racism

self-haters and on the other end Martin Luther King and the colour blind advocates of the Enlightenment.

There is an added problem with this praise of the colourful, mostly affecting the masochist nationalist. It has to do with collectivist affection, and its relation to the rights of the autonomous individual. While certain religious degrading clothing, such as the Muslim burqa, fits into a colourful society, the burqa itself is not colourful in the least. It is an image suited at great distance for Western expatriates at the sight of fully covered women who are paying the price for Western self-congratulatory diversity.

A final comment about those "colourful" societies and the racist assumptions they all seem to be troubled by. The question is whether or not you would put the safety of your own country ahead of the safety of distant countries marred by conflict and social unrest. To the positive nationalist, of course, it is always "your country first." Cultures overseas come second if at all, and if you disagree, he says I don't mind. Masochist nationalists, then, at least at first sight, have a completely different opinion. They pride themselves of always putting the interest of countries overseas ahead of their own country which they fail to appreciate anyway. Nationalist self-obsession, they maintain, is unforgivable. But the reasons behind their type of "colourful" society seem to speak a different language. We saw above how weary they were to disclose any more troublesome traits within their overseas' culture of emotional identification because this "might play into the hands of populists domestically." No conflict in the culture where they have sunk their personality, then, is allowed to fuel political polarization at home – spearheaded by, worth repeating – a party the ominous character of which has been invented by the masochist nationalists themselves. Real, grave political problems elsewhere, then, cannot trump their own fabricated political pessimism at home. This doesn't go well, it seems, with their proudly announced anti-nationalist principles. Rather, they seem to agree on "your country first," even though their way of getting there is more psychologically intricate compared to the blunt egotism of a positive nationalist. One vividly admits that task number one is to prevent mounting class tensions from the left domestically, and another – at least if you take a closer look – is obsessively engaged in preventing political unrest domestically coming from the right. The nationalist interest prevails while both types of nationalist care little about suffering in distant cultures. Racism within positive nationalism appears indistinguishable from racism within masochist nationalism.

Whites only! Blacks only!

When it comes to racial segregation, positive nationalists are caught by nostalgia for more intimate days when race-mixing was uncommon and bars and park benches announced "Whites only." All of this, of course, makes any masochist nationalist shudder, and others too. Still, caught by *the obscurantist temptation* as

Caroline Fourest calls one of her books, the opportunities of segregation has left a fatal impression on them.[16] Molefi Asante is one of the most famous spokespersons for "Afrocentricity," the political method discussed earlier where the perspective of the "African person" is being celebrated and cherished. "Of course," Asante maintains, "segregation was legally and morally wrong, but something was given to black children in those schools that was just as important in some senses as the new books, better educated teachers, and improved buildings of this era. The children were centred in cultural ways that made learning interesting and intimate."[17]

New books, educated teachers and modern facilities, Asante implies, may not make up for the benefits of a black person. This is nostalgia – racial idealization of black people – a kind of "Blacks only!" sign concerning education of coloured children. While it all may be surrounded by caring smiles, it is depressingly anti-intellectual and pessimistic. Blacks and whites must be kept apart. Jean-Marie Le Pen spoke about ethno-pluralism, a kind of pluralism behind barbed wire supposedly defending French values. We have been trained to abhor this. But what is the difference between positive nationalists fending off an outsider, and ethno-mysticism along the lines of the troubled masochist nationalist?

Positive nationalists become nostalgic about the old times of "Whites only," and masochist nationalists become nostalgic about the old days of "Blacks only." While the former mocks intellectuals and shun formal qualifications for the benefit of *Blut und Boden*, the latter becomes emotional about native teachers and their indigenous wisdom. Both of them hold deeply conservative views and prefer the company of one's own kind. Skin colour makes learning more interesting. But you cannot escape racial segregation by replacing negative stereotypes with positive ones. From the point of view of principle, it is no different if you wish to fend off whites from the lives of black people or the other way around. In both cases it is all about amassing all things exotic into a cage of colourful splendour for us Westerners to marvel at – either on our high horses in horror and astonishment, or in post-imperialist shame, envy and fascination.

Numerous advocates of "Afrocentricity" such as Asante have a background in Africa. Do they still fit into the scheme of Western masochist nationalist? Or should they rather be seen as native Africans and hence as everyday positive nationalists favouring their own culture while belittling the West where they hold an academic position? The question is not trivial, as it further blurs the border between positive and masochist nationalists.

We can take this observation a bit further. If we imagine those Western masochist nationalists where they'd rather like to be, say, on Cuba, the mirror image is no longer there. In front of us, instead, we have an ordinary positive nationalist looking down on anything foreign while getting all emotional about Cuban identity. This is important to add because, I believe, it shows that the only difference between our two nationalists is that one of them is busy over there and the other one is busy over here.

110 Racism

As I have tried to show throughout this discussion, the gist of positive nationalism is not scientific. Rather, the emphasis is on optical and aesthetic qualities along the lines of racial classification such as physiognomy and skin colour. From this point of view, we instantly experience a sense of community – or animosity – at the mere sight of each other. Words have little meaning. From a progressive and intellectualist point of view, the only way to counter this primitivist definition of community is to refuse to recognise people until they speak, not unlike, in fact, closing your eyes.

Masochist nationalists, however, are equally obsessed by these racial, superficial differences. In their eyes we are silent exhibitionists displaying our colourful ethnic exterior. We have come a long way from Simone Weil's grey dress drawing attention to her mind, and classic socialists agitating in shirt and trousers. Masochist nationalism makes us slightly less human and a bit more like animals. Two forms of nationalism are pulling in the same direction.

Racist name-calling - Niggers and white trash

Another similarity between positive and masochist nationalists is a tendency towards racist name-calling. While the accusations fly in opposite direction, the carelessness and lack of nuances are basically the same. There is a middle position of classic liberals and reformist left-wingers where racist slurs are uncommon, but nationalists are too insensitive not having a laugh at the expense of vulnerable groups among their opponents. Starting with positive nationalists, racist name-calling against non-whites are too many to mention. An Iraqi suspected of criminal activity is an "Ali baba." A "house negro" was someone who was hired under slave-like conditions. "Victor Charlie" (VC) was Vietnam War military slang for Viet Cong, and "coolie" was an unskilled Asian labourer. "Jim crow," "Northern monkey," "Blue-gum," "Ape," "Uncle Tom," and "Jungle bunny" is a black person, and "Towel head" is a Hindu. Towering over all of them, of course, is that racist crown jewel – "nigger."

These racist slurs all have a rough, slightly unsophisticated bent, and those who are still around are confined to the far right-wing scene. No one with a public reputation would use them. Right-wingers rarely understand the predicament of others. We call it "social circumstances" – conditions out of your control. An expression such as "Jungle bunny" is only possible if you – whether out of ignorance or sheer malice – ignore that some people are homeless because of fate and do not share the privileges of a positive nationalist. It comes very naturally to oppose racist name-calling. Social circumstances rule out racist slurs in any direction. But as we turn to masochist nationalists they do not seem to go all the way – or rather they do from the view of emotional determination. But in terms of political principle, they have moved very little. Rigorous political consistency, it seems, is trumped by vengeance and ideology.

While lashing out against racist slurs from the opposite camp, masochist nationalists use racist name-calling when it suits their own ideological interests with no sense of inner ambiguity. "Rednecks," "white trash," "trailer-park trash" "voting cattle" and "herd of voters," all suggests unskilled white people, low on income and education voting on Donald Trump. From German we have the term "Modernisierungsverlierer" (losers in the process of modernization), implying people with a blank passport left behind in the tech-race. Hillary Clinton famously said half of Trump's voters belonged to "the basket of deplorables."[18]

The term "white trash" is racist because it creates a prejudiced stereotype of Caucasians. It also refers to marginalised people as garbage – who not long ago were called unemployed, workers, or the proletariat evoking left-wing compassion. The less tech-savvy are deemed ignorant and will go astray politically. Individuals voting right-wing are sheep or cows to be educated into voting on the identity left. Only workers who vote as they should make an informed choice. The ignorant disciple, then, is insightful, while the well-read critic is deemed ill-informed. This attack against the right is religious in all but name.

Individuals without a proper home are labelled "trailer-park trash." Above, there was no end to the excuses on behalf of homeless individuals from overseas, and no criticism was spared against positive nationalist name-calling. Now, there is no end to racist name-calling against homeless groups in the US. They are the Jungle Bunnies of the West. I don't mind a racist joke, but never on our expense, says the positive nationalist, and only on our expense, says the masochist nationalists – two manifestations of partisan ideological propaganda. Social circumstances for us, and merciless essentialism for others. Positive nationalists said "niggers" should not be allowed to vote. Expatriates in the United Nations say "white trash" supporting Trump should not be allowed to vote. "Who votes for Trump anyway?" an elegant French lady exclaimed in an upmarket fish restaurant in Hanoi. "Well, he won the election," didn't he? I said, spoiling the dinner.

One should not, however, ignore differences between these two nationalisms. Racist slurs by positive nationalists, we noted above, often appear unrefined and limited to outer traits or cheap jokes such as an elaborate turban seen as a towel. It is always racist, but seldom political. Racist invectives from the camp of self-abasing nationalists, however, appear more sophisticated. It is all racist, and mostly political. References to elections and why "voting cattle" should be barred from participating is more common among masochist nationalists, as if academics are mostly behind them. While racist name-calling against marginalised groups overseas appear to emanate from below – i.e. from similar outsiders in the West, racist slurs against destitute groups in the West originate, so it seems, from above. They are a mark of sophistication within the Western elites.

Unfair allegations – Nazis and revolutionaries

Above, we saw how both positive and masochist nationalists lapse into divisive name calling against vulnerable groups among their adversaries. This hostile tendency not only, however, target destitute groups. It also homes in on those

112 Racism

who are politically active in either camp. They do this for, at least, two reasons. First, to silence dissent, and second, to frighten the public with political horror scenarios. Positive nationalists, to start with, were always inclined to radicalise any opinion among one's critics. Any deviation from capitalism was called revolutionary, and its advocates – often reformist socialists or liberals – were branded "thugs" and "criminals" claiming to seek a communist overthrow of society, while the general population was expected to tremble at the sight of the state taken over by left-wing radicals and international riff-raff. At the same time, dissenters were punished. Salaries were cut, and colleagues had complaints. Mistakes had been made. Perhaps they lost their jobs or were thrown in jail. The critic, it was plain to see, should be silenced.

Masochist nationalists in power, however, also tend to radicalise statements of adversaries. Any political act of deviation from identity politics will be deemed "racist." If you wonder why two weekly SAS flights are carrying a thousand Iranian political refugees holiday return ticket Stockholm – Teheran, "xenophobe," "fascist" or even "Nazi" might come your way, even though you merely think political asylum should be for those who can never go back home again – and the Swedish population is expected to tremble at the thought of marching right-wingers. Also, critics will be punished. A pay rise may not happen. Colleagues will talk, and you'll be called in for consultations. The union representative is slow, and the next week he is appointed Head of Department. The critic must be silenced. UN expatriates in their office overseas cannot bring to attention the fact that local staff do their nails on office hours for fear of being labelled "Xenophobes." The entire UN adheres to self-censorship and the "racism of low expectations," because we must expect less, they believe, from local staff.

While one type of nationalist invents an exotic riff raff to tame and lure the public into submission under conservative oppression, the other type of nationalist manufactures a band of home-grown racists to usher the people into compliance with political correctness and globalization. They are saying very different things and they would disagree until their dying days, but in terms of underlying worldview they have a lot in common.

Not only does the masochist nationalist with surprising ease use racist slurs against political opponents. He also puts himself in the same political corner. "You're a racist." he will tell you unless you pay attention, "and, by the way, I'm a racist, too." We are back at the previous job interview where the two academics did not miss an opportunity to unite in shame along with skinheads who had murdered a black man. What is the point of accusations if you are also affected by them? During times of peace, Friedrich Nietzsche notes, the warrior hurls the dagger into his own belly.

Ideological stereotyping

Throughout history, non-Western cultures have suffered from patronising stereotypes by Western imperialists. Next to "Blue-gum," "Nigger" and other racist epithets above, entire generations from overseas have been written off as "foolish," "hopeless," "uninteresting" or – graciously – as "underperformers." As a block of dark intruders, they brought ruin and undermined democracy. It was all condescension and hatred based on nothing but racism and cultural sadism.

Masochist nationalists, then, set out to erase ideological stereotyping the way Western imperialists were doing it. Cultural hierarchies must be prevented in any direction. But somewhere along the way, masochist nationalists were led astray by their own conviction. They had forgotten that ideological stereotyping was the menace and Western imperialism merely an expression of it. Instead, they overlooked the troublesome underlying principle and went after the manifestation of the moment greeted by an equally confused left-wing audience. Below, this fatal shift of attention will be illustrated by two telling cases – a political brochure and an ambitious tourist leaflet – both from Germany.

In a brochure published by the German Green Party, strangers are collectively described as "positive potential" and we approach them with a sense of "fascination." The "democratic maturity of a society," the leaflet proudly adds, "is only manifested in the interaction with strangers."[19] How, then, is positive potential to be understood? As a glorifying stereotype whereby the presence of any overseas culture has a range of positive consequences.

The test of this abstract generosity is to apply it on something more familiar. If focus is shifted towards Europe, the idea of a "positive potential" no longer appears vaguely uplifting, but puzzling, almost like a misprint. Few would, for instance, label Belgians a "positive potential," because we don't know all of them. Belgians, to us, are individuals, faces, names. The warm, all-embracing idea suddenly stands out as aloof and grotesquely collectivist. It rests on our ignorance, perhaps indifference. They are faceless – hence they may be hailed but also scorned. Opinions about animals are opinions about the group and not about a particular animal, as in I prefer dogs to cats. Similarly, masochist nationalist veneration of the exotic is not based on specific individuals, but on "the Other" as a species or even a race. These racist implications loom under a thin veil of multicultural anti-racism, and this shows another disquieting parallel with positive nationalism. Whether we label them as a "positive" or a "negative" potential we make use of stereotypes from the 1930s. In Malmö, the south-Swedish city infamous for ongoing multicultural turmoil, the government is trying to combat "xenophobia" with state-run projects by the name of "Xenofili! – We love foreigners." Two types of ideological stereotyping emerge: Positive nationalist "phobia" is mirrored by masochist nationalist "philia."

For the sake of empathy or admiration, masochist nationalists put those from overseas on a pedestal. We down here. They up there. Masochist nationalism flickers between blind enthusiasm and suffocating pity, not unlike a postcolonial upper class soothing its conscience with humanistic jargon. The stranger is different, original or awkward, clumsy or fascinating, virile or

114 Racism

ethereal, victim or Jack-of-all-trades. Either we admire their superiority or feel emotional about their suffering. Carefully, they are removed from our community and made into our delight and objects of our opinions and discriminations. We make sure they are not lost in the crowd because this would be tantamount to oppression and majority violence, and to render them invisible. Instead we acknowledge them, and they feel acknowledged, and we approach "the Other" in "a conversation across cultural borders" sterile as salicylic cotton. We single them out, make them special, unique, one of a kind – in other words subject them to exclusion. When "the Other" is seen as "an object and as something completely without self-determination" an "imperialist attitude can be maintained."[20] At the end of the day, this masochist nationalist selection and division is a racist practice. No matter in what direction, whether we opt for patronising or eulogising ideological stereotyping, the stranger is doomed to be different.

In the German Green Party brochure above, we are also advised to approach strangers with a sense of "fascination." Again, we seem far away from positive nationalist patronising stereotypes. But it is a stereotype nevertheless and the similarity with their antagonists' stereotyping indifference or even revulsion is more apparent than we think. In fact, fascination constitutes a political baseline for racist sentiments. Racism is the emotional climax in a situation where the stranger has been deprived of his resemblance with us; i.e. of his human nature. We are human beings; those who differ from us are not human beings. Racism does not rule out fascination. Racism is fascination of a certain kind. To be held in contempt, something must first be acknowledged. Displaying one's sexual, ethnic or other traits is not risk-free. Racism is fascination taken to its logical conclusion. The masochist nationalist fails to notice the inherent worth of disinterestedness, to blend in and vanish in the crowd – which, by the way, puts a political question mark not only around fascination but also around "interest" or even "attention." The multiculturalist has abandoned Martin Luther King's "colour-blind society," believing you can fight racism by preaching it from the other end. At this point, masochist nationalism blends with positive nationalism. It does not matter whether strangers are portrayed as victims, heroes or villains, as long as a postmodern image of "us-and-them" is upheld, where they are subject of exclusion and exoticism – put on the pedestal to be honoured, scorned, or drenched with pity.

This sense of fascination, moreover, is not the result of knowledge, because knowledge leads to scepticism and rules out wide-eyed, naïve fascination. The more you know, the less room for unchecked emotions and wild generalizations. If you're in Addis Ababa, you know Mulugeta is different from Sarah. In fact, they quarrel. Behind this self-abasing fascination lies ignorance, and it cannot survive first-hand knowledge. "I know enough of the working-class not to idealise it," George Orwell said after the time he spent in the mid-England mining districts in preparation for *The Road to Wigan Pier.* Whether the object of your political passions are under-privileged groups at home or exotic cultures, fascination requires little knowledge but all the more imagination, and the more experience you have, the less you are inclined to engage in glorifying stereotypes. "As I said apropos of Galsworthy," Orwell continues,

> The opinions of the sentimentalist change into their opposites at the first thought of reality. Scratch the average pacifist and you find a jingo. The middle-class ILP'er (International Labour Party'er) and the bearded fruit-juice drinker are all for a classless society so long as they see the proletariat through the wrong end of the telescope; force them into any real contact with a proletarian – let them get into a fight with a drunken fish-porter on Saturday night, for instance – and they are capable of swinging back to the most ordinary middle-class snobbishness.[21]

Orwell delivers a hard blow to this kind of empty left-wing fascination. Unless maintained by ignorance, it may suddenly re-emerge as middle-class arrogance. While virtue is lost, honesty, perhaps, is acquired.

Moreover, what happens if you have been trained and taught to be "fascinated" at the sight of anything foreign? A positive nationalist always reacts with indifference, sometimes even distaste. Interestingly enough, similarities emerge between these two forms of ideological stereotyping. If you approach strangers with preconceived animosity, they are helpless. Whatever they say or do, you are indifferent. No matter how they suffer, your look is distant, often hostile. If you instead approach strangers with a sense of fascination, little has changed. They are equally helpless and at the mercy of your pre-conceived verdict. Whatever they do, your reaction is predetermined. If they are hungry, you are fascinated. If they violate the law, you are fascinated, and fold your fingers in a love message.[22] Whether you are repelled or fascinated you're uninterested in who they are, because you have made up your mind, no matter what. From two ends, the positive and the masochist nationalist meet in ideological stereotyping of overseas' individuals. The liberal, unassuming approach in the middle free from prejudices and idealizations, where strangers and others are assessed depending on what they say or do, appears out of reach for both type of nationalist.

The final quote of interest in this Green Party leaflet has to do with the "democratic maturity of a society," which, the leaflet says, "is only manifested in the interaction with strangers." Again, at least on the surface, we are witnessing a powerful vindication of right-wing stereotyping, saying something like "democracy will be undermined unless you keep borders closed." The key to democracy is not us but them. When a society's democratic acumen, then, is only sparked by engaging with strangers, its own citizens getting together is an empty activity, at least from the point of view of boosting democracy.

But what does this mean? Clearly, it is good for any society's "democratic maturity" – as high sounding as it looks – to socialise with "strangers." But why would it be a prerequisite? What is the nature of that democratic essence that

116 Racism

mysteriously comes about only when you engage with people you have never met before? If non-whites are assigned some innate humane qualities spreading prosperity, are we not, then, back in the arms of that ogre of racial hierarchies? Isn't the true test of democracy the way citizens interact regardless of "background," talk with anybody, and see who has the best argument – which, by the way, requires a common mental framework – excluding "strangers?" Positive nationalists say democracy is strengthened by their own esteemed culture of preference only, and this is also what masochist nationalists are saying, as patrons on behalf of their far-off culture of spiritual identification. These are two cases of ideological stereotyping.

These self-degrading ideas of "democratic maturity" from afar can also be applied on those exotic cultures so favoured by masochist nationalists. These cultures, we are told, must be protected from the undermining impact of the West. But haven't we just been taught democratic maturity only shows when you socialise with strangers? In case a Koran teacher would fail to see a tall, atheist European as an opportunity to increase their political maturity, would the Koran teacher, then, qualify as far right-winger? The question appears to leave the masochist nationalist with no way out. Either, he accepts the principle that stranger only fuel democracy and the shimmer around his exoticism is gone forever – or he dismisses it, and his rhetoric about democratic maturity is gone with the wind.

But the entire rhetoric has little to do with the extent to which an abstract "stranger" reveals a community's democratic maturity. It all boils down to the masochist nationalist principle: We are not to be trusted. We are a negative potential. We must consult individuals from outside the Western hemisphere because otherwise our culture will succumb from democratic immaturity. Exotic cultures are to be trusted. They must not consult strangers, because if they do their cultures will be undermined and disintegrate into something less politically accountable, less real and less wholesome. Cultures that have gone through the steel bath of Marxism and religious reformation, passed the acid test of Enlightenment and modernity, where conservative structures such as trust in blind authority and lack of free speech have been successfully countered – these cultures are naïve, not to be trusted unless they are rescued by someone from overseas. Cultures haunted by blind authority, lack of free speech, suppression of women, corruption, war, genocide and waves of emigration as in 2016, must never be suffused and perverted by, for instance, a German engineer who, perhaps, could help improving the Dar Es Salaam bus station. This is masochist nationalism in practise – multicultural self-hatred and the infatuation with the exotic.

The second case of ideological stereotyping is found in the spring edition of *Stadtrevue*, the tourist leaflet of the German city of Köln. "All whites are racists," the front page said, perhaps an daring title if you wish to attract visitors to the city. We have touched upon the phrase before. Here, however, we shall only say a few words about it from the viewpoint of racist stereotyping. The question is: Are positive nationalists saying something different?

"All whites are racists" could well be a global watchword among masochist nationalists. Nothing is easier than using this unforgiving generalization against white people, as shown by Black Lives Matter in 2020. This opinion about white people is a moral end station. On this side of it, there are many opportunities for self-criticism. The situation for migrants, for instance, is not perfect. But in the eyes of a self-humiliating political enthusiast, these nuances are a betrayal of the cause and almost like sleeping with the enemy – the positive nationalist. He, in turn, would claim all blacks are primitive and uncivilised. This verdict is a moral end station. You could bring up problems related to black people without going to the extreme, but positive nationalists see no reason to be social workers. Their doom over black people, however, does not seem to be true because if it was, positive nationalists would not be amused by it, as they seem to be, but rather afraid. Masochist nationalists' ideological stereotyping about "all whites are racists" is also most likely made up, because if this was true, the streets would be teeming with brown-shirts and any "anti-racist" would be in trouble. Rather, it is merely self-harassing entertainment. One fictitious racist propaganda stands against another made-up racist propaganda. One says whites are inferior, the other one says blacks are inferior – two manifestations of ideological stereotyping.

Virulent nationalism and neo-liberalism

In the final discussion, we shall describe how this racist-inspired interest in visual traits above, common among both manifestations of nationalism, is leading onwards to another shared point of reference – neo-liberalism. First, an illustration of this trajectory of ideas within masochist nationalism, mirrored, subsequently, by similar political linkages within positive nationalism.

Recently, I saw a TV-commercial, where individuals from a distant land – I believe it was Thailand – were performing advanced dance rituals, swinging rods and the like. The speed of the images was very high. We were somehow back in the era of motionless pictures, as the impression of breakneck pace was due to constantly new snaps of imagery. It was all very colourful and all very superficial. Whatever it was about, it was not about Thailand.

It struck me, though, as I was watching these vivid images flashing by, that they reminded me of the ways in which exotic ethnic minorities are being portrayed by masochist nationalists. Watching the speed and the carnival of disconnected images and the lack of any scent of real life beyond the glossy surface, it was as if the dead and yet superficially enticing imagery of masochist nationalism had suddenly come to life right in front of me. I realised why these politically correct, upbeat descriptions of far-off lands were so familiar. They were already everywhere – in the form of colourful TV-commercials. I understood why I was rarely caught by that kind of cultural enthusiasm. It was, I felt, a smile hinting at your wallet. Masochist nationalism is singularly focused on the exterior; bodies, skin colour, hairstyle, clothes, jawbone, the shape of the skull – and the world of commercialism is obsessed with the same things. Masochist nationalism is the academic version of make-up – L'Oréal with a footnote. In stereotypical advertisements for exotic cultures, filled with dancing, singing and laughing, with rods and sticks in all colours imaginable thrown about, at this point of intense fascination for seductive form and superficial aesthetics, masochist nationalism blends with neo-liberalism. The entire idea of pluralism and diversity, richness, and perhaps even the very notion of wealth, is being hijacked by masochist nationalists and neoliberals; an alliance between an absolutely confused left, and an absolutely determined right.

Positive nationalists are engaged in something different and still very similar. As a result of their indifference to cultures overseas, real interest is traded for entertainment – festivals, displays of popular culture and perhaps tense, half-hearted appreciation of dancing dervishes aspiring for material poverty, offering an excuse for positive nationalists' own affluence. It is all superficial and inauthentic, hard to distinguish from the colourful TV-commercial above.

Positive nationalists prefer cheap excitement because they just want to be entertained and are not really interested in what's behind, and masochist nationalists prefer cheap excitement because they are afraid of what's behind. Whether it is fuelled by collectivist enthusiasm or by collectivist lack of interest, the result in both cases is a preference for shallow cultural images hard to distinguish from the commercial messages of neo-liberalism.

Notes

1 Webster, 1997, p. 82.
2 "Médecins Sans Frontières is 'institutionally racist,' say 1,000 insiders."
3 Frankell, 30 September, 2014.
4 Kowalsky, 1992, p. 116.
5 Webster, 1997, p. 30
6 Diop, 1974, pp. 2-3.
7 "Inledande bestämmelser".
8 Webster, 1997, p. 85.
9 Lombroso, 1911, pp. xiv-xv.
10 Ibid., p. 6.
11 Orwell, 2001, Ch. 7.
12 Webster, 1997, p. 34.
13 Kowalsky, 1992, p. 116.
14 Bawer, 2006, p. 51.
15 Ibid.
16 Fourest, 2005.
17 Asande, p. 29.
18 "Hillary Clinton Calls Many Trump Backers 'Deplorables,' and G.O.P. Pounces", 10 September, 2016.
19 Kowalsky, 1992, p. 119.
20 Friedman, 2007, p. 437.

21 Orwell, 2001, p. 151.

22 In the early 1990s, at a dinner with the Swedish PEN-Association in honor of Taslima Nasrin, who had just been awarded Writer in Residence in Stockholm, I started comparing the brief, erratic life of a human being with the long, calm existence of the dinner plates surrounding us on the table, sometimes stretching many hundreds of years. Isn't it annoying and arrogant? I asked Nasrin. She laughed at the thought, grabbed a number of plates, sat down on the floor and started smashing them one by one against the wooden tiles. The interesting thing, however, was the reaction around me. The air was calm, almost serene. Nobody raised their voice. Nobody looked at Nasrin, and yet they all did. Conversations continued, but now they had something tense about them, con- stituted, I thought, at the plates being crushed one by one by an international literary celebrity. Eventually, the hostess slowly walked over to Nasrin and gently twisted the next plate to come out of her hands. While a commoner at once had protested and grabbed the plates out of her hands - celebrity or not - she was now, presumably, rescued by the fact that she was surrounded by Westerners who, despite being members of the International PEN-Association, still had their senses partly blurred by masochist nationalism, according to which plates going down on the floor at the hands of an exotic literary celebrity still, somehow, must have something elevated and gracious about it.

12

A LIBERAL WAY OUT OF NATIONALIST OSSIFICATION?

In this discussion, we have seen how two manifestations of nationalism are engaged in a never-ending conflict, where the interests and passions of "our" culture is advocated to the detriment of other cultures. It is a political echo-chamber with, as it seems, no way out. The book could end here, on a disquieting note, suspended eternally, as it were, between positive and masochist nationalism. Below, however, we shall point towards a possible way out of this nationalist impasse. It is informed by classic liberal values. Throughout these closing pages, it will be argued that the proposed way out is very different from any masochist nationalist counter measure against positive nationalism. It is an alternative of kind, not of degree. The entire frequency of misconceived nationalist antagonism, then, would be abandoned for the sake of political principles and real disagreement and conflict. Therefore, we will now briefly reiterate those themes above, trying to suggest a liberal way out of nationalist ossification.

Both manifestations of nationalism claim the pre-eminence of the roots where they have sunk their personality, while dismissing the roots of others. Roots and history, a liberal would claim, are important for everyone. There is no hierarchy and, as Johann Herder said, there is no Favoritenvolk. Roots are authentic everywhere or nowhere. Confusion or even boredom at the sight of exotic cultures is more respectful than faked enthusiasm. Whatever you do, says George Orwell, acknowledge your privileges. Roots is not fascism, but a sense of belonging. Cultural self-respect is not cultural self-obsession.

Nationalists either belittle overseas languages, or their own language. The only way to come closer to a truly liberal, internationalist approach, however, is to dismiss cheap cultural supremacy and let people enjoy and protect their respective languages. Nobody is a prisoner of a culture. Everyone should have access to the international arena of technology and progress. This is not the exclusive territory of Westerners. While masochist nationalists seek refuge in bourgeois conformism and playing to the crowd, they accuse the dissident heading for the depths of culture for being a fascist. Positive nationalists – from the other end – capitalise on originality and sacrifice, brutalising it into facets of fascism. Instead, we could adhere to the Enlightenment and the virtue of dissent, independence, and creativity as a bulwark against groupthink whether bourgeois or fascist.

If you embrace any culture with kitschy images, you ought to make practical changes in your life in that direction. Otherwise, a liberal would insist, you are merely a theorist and a coward, trying to acquire political bona fide by comparing your own culture unfavourably to other cultures. Positive nationalists are not troubled by it because their culture of adulation is their own. They love their own country and also live in it. Enthusiasm for an overseas' culture, a liberal would insist, should be supported by knowledge. The combination of poor knowledge and excitement is at heart a religious idea. Historical kitsch is bad everywhere. Ethnic self-importance, a liberal would maintain, is no better than big-headed nationalism.

Afrocentric history books mirror Eurocentric ones. But history books are not supposed to instil a sense of grandeur or animosity or old-school sectarianism cloaked as minority rights. History books should tell the truth within the frames of open ideological controversy. The only way to counter group privileges is to oppose the principle of group selection. If the supremacy of one group is merely traded for the rule of another group, nothing has been achieved. If we respond by means of a principle, we cannot escape from books favouring one region by putting the magnifying glass elsewhere, but only by refusing to use a magnifying glass altogether.

Memory is one thing, obsession with one's past another. If citizens have to reschedule their morning routines, it does not matter whether streets are blocked by Western or Eastern religious fanatics commemorating a battle from the past. The liberal way out of this paralysing historical infatuation is to learn how to forget, let go, and forgive in order to live and act in the present and in the future.

Both manifestations of nationalism are characterised by group fanaticism. The individual is crushed into a mere exponent of a culture, and the greater the overlap between individual and culture, the safer, it is claimed, the individual. But from the point of view of individual liberty, safety in imprisonment makes a mockery of safety. The charismatic populist leader carried forth on the shoulders of a silent, grateful crowd is mirrored by the charismatic ethnic representative speaking on behalf of his down-beaten compatriots. In this scheme, any spokesperson can represent his entire community regardless of political opinions. The way to exit this apolitical group fanaticism is to insist on the integrity of the individual, and, following late 18th-century Paris, the pre-eminence of political assemblies above communities based on religion, clan or tribe.

Extremists on the right say people are different in order to single out groups for extermination. Masochist nationalists say people are different in order to show recognition and compassion, or so they think, and positive nationalists

122 Liberal way out of nationalist ossification

instantly agree because they wish to preserve economic difference and injustice. One says we are different and superior, and another says we are different and inferior. The classic social democratic or liberal way out of the dangerous allure of difference is to dismiss it altogether for the benefit of the welfare state, of similarities, equalities, true, close-up understanding, and the virtues of anonymity and vanishing into the crowd. Cross-ethnic solidarity trumps any "diversity" and cultural self-obsession confined to the walls of ethnicity.

From the tribunes in parliament, right-wingers say left-wing artists belong in jail, and left-wingers say this is akin to National Socialism. Right-wing artists are jailed by left-wingers, and right-wingers say left-wingers act like Nazis. But if you don't like it, the pluralist Lars Vilks says, don't look at it. Whether things exist or not should be decided by those who favour it, and not by those who oppose it. The principle of artistic freedom stands above ideology. Masochist nationalists always pretend to defend freedom of the arts, while, in practice, they rarely do. Their fall in grace is greater. The progressive motto L'art pour l'art ought to be reinstalled in the art discussion. Positive nationalists never knew about it, and masochist nationalists have replaced it with concern for minorities. If political art is not provocative, radical artists agreed in the 1920s, it is not political. Empty provocations are better than any political straight-jacket. Artistic rebellion is never right-wing extreme. It is defined by its radical opposition to power. When the elite is colonised by the left, the left not only becomes elitist, but conservative as well, seeking status quo and to cling on to its privileges.

While positive nationalists favour their own kind, masochist nationalists take it to the other extreme and at the same do very little: they claim "hate crime" only relates to their exotic group of emotional identification. From the point of view of a political principle, however, both approaches must be abandoned for the benefit of equality and meritocracy. Nothing has been achieved, if privileges are merely handed over from one group to another group.

Ethnic discrimination is being mystified in both manifestations of nationalism. While positive nationalists say any injustice against any one of us is a violation against all of us, masochist nationalists, as in a political house of mirrors, maintain any injustice against any member of an exotic culture violates his culture as a whole. Both manifestations of nationalism gloss over any disruptive class antagonism for the benefit of permanent elite dominance. The left-wing aura surrounding masochist nationalism cannot survive. Expose, a Marxist would suggest, the underlying class oppression behind any pseudo-leftist rhetoric about minority emancipation. The individual ought to be reinstalled at centre stage of analysis, while the frames of culture are partly taken down and demystified. This case of mystification goes even further. Unless economic discrimination contains a cultural component, both exponent of nationalism might ignore it altogether. We must take off those distorting spectacles of ethnicity and nationalism, a pluralist would insist, and realise what was once uncontroversial political knowledge: exploitation and discrimination do not have a qualifying tag on them. They may be cultural, national, racial, or, most commonly, political and economic, based on class conflict.

While positive nationalists see no problem violating the sovereignty of other nations, masochist nationalists welcome the intrusion of foreign ideas, such as Sharia laws, into their own country. Both exponent of nationalism would endorse sanctions against cultures they dislike but be against it regarding cultures they approve of. There is, however, a liberal principle at work, although it might not be approved by all of those who claim to be liberals. The principle says that sanctions rarely work. As a rule, any infringement upon any sovereign state will radicalise the population and strengthen conservative opposition to foreign intrusion and to the international community at large. If you fail to acknowledge this conservative knee-jerk reaction, you are most likely also a conservative.

An argument, according to the principle of meritocracy, should be assessed based on its own qualities, as text on paper. Neither manifestation of nationalism, however, treasure this principle. Either, they are under the impression that power is an argument in itself, and, if need be, can be further underpinned by a spark of emotions; or they claim that powerlessness as such is an argument, which, in addition, may be supported by violent display of emotions. Some say "we had it coming," others say "they had it coming," but we all make choices, and are responsible for them. Violence can never be excused by destiny or determinism. In the past, law was subjective and spoke the voice of the oppressor. Now, Western legislation tends to be subjective on the side of "the oppressed." According to liberal, modern jurisdiction, however, court decisions must rest on both accounts and try to find out what actually happened out there.

Societal pessimism is at the core of any radical political ideology. Here, the two manifestations of nationalism are one. They both keep accusing one particular group, whether it goes under the name of xenophobia, or oikophobia – unjustified fear of homeland. Due to their pessimism, they both unite as one collective bloc, some in anger to magnify aggression against others, others in shame and arousal to share the blame for right-wing atrocities against foreigners. Whether self-conscious or disheartened about it, both positive and masochist nationalists claim to be racists. Instead of engaging in a proper argument (which they might lose), they make use of all their sentimental pet phrases such as abuse, insult, and blasphemy, whether the culture under their wings is their own or an exotic culture. Hence, they transform the classic argument into a case for law enforcement and violate the heritage of the Enlightenment. Instead of uniting in anger or in shame, we should try to avoid it altogether, and insist on the individual as political baseline. Finally, instead of being thin-skinned and lack emotional restraint, we may be grateful to the critic, as J. S. Mill reminded us. Either, the critic is wrong, and we had to find out – or he is right, and we have acquired new knowledge for free.

Positive nationalists see no reason to share their wealth because of a sense of superiority and reason and logic in it. Masochist nationalist are ungenerous as a result of their sense of inferiority – we have our own problems. Under the cloak,

124 Liberal way out of nationalist ossification

they are only two paths to the same goal: moral self-importance and a chilling indifference. A liberal, then, would not deny our superiority, but point out the overwhelming aspect of luck and good fortune in it – at least as individuals. Non-Western cultures are often inferior, which, a liberal (and Marxist) would add, does not mean that individuals from overseas are inferior. Rather, the more acute the situation, the more urgent calls for change. This joint recognition of societal hierarchies and individual innocence, a liberal and Marxist would agree, is the political engine behind any transformation and liberation. Positive nationalists never admitted it, and masochist nationalists have managed to suppress it for the benefit of voyeuristic cultural recognition.

Our two manifestations of nationalism have an equally sectarian and reactionary approach to humour. Both of them are short fused about "their" culture. Incapable of scientific detachment, they throw their stakes on one side or other, and start inventing majestic justifications around "their cause." The liberal John Rawls "veil of ignorance" may offer an alternative. Standing behind this veil, you are asked to suggest the set-up of a good society without knowing your own place in it. Both of them would fail in this endeavour. We must openly counter these wildly emotional reactions from either side and call them by their real name, as "exaggerated," "out-of-proportion," "immature," or "childish." Ever since the Enlightenment, we have learned to listen to people only when they produce a coherent argument, and not when they lost their temper. "(I)rascibility on insufficient cause, and resentment disproportioned to the provocation," J. S. Mill said, "These are moral vices, and constitute a bad and odious moral character."[1] To be prone to instant aggression, like our two nationalists, defines, says Mill, an unpleasant character, which leads us to wonder whether concessions in either direction is really worthwhile. But there is more to it. Research tells us that people with a sense of humour and irony are smarter, as their minds are constantly at work on different levels on the lookout for simultaneous, perhaps opposing interpretations of reality. What we are witnessing, a liberal conversationalist might maintain, is the revolt of the humourless, heavy-handed nationalist against those who stand in the tradition of Voltaire and Mill, with elegance, culture, and wit.

Both positive and masochist nationalism contain a seed of death cult, where life's purpose does not lie in life on earth, but in the here-after. While positive nationalists, heirs in the fascist pantheon, support sacrifices for political utopia, Muslim suicide bombers, heading for religious utopia, are backed by masochist nationalists. While fighting for different or perhaps opposite objectives, they are both equally replete with political romanticism – such as heroic nihilism and death cult. Rather than facing our emptiness they turn to wishful thinking. There is a secular way out of this. According to science, there is no heaven. Life may be better if we abandon any utopian vision for the benefits of small, careful social steps and accomplishments. As the liberal philosopher Karl Popper maintained in The Open Society and Its Enemies, we should turn from the careless leap into the unknown by the name of "utopian social engineering," towards

Liberal way out of nationalist ossification   **125**

careful, step-by-step "piecemeal social engineering" with life on earth in mind.[2] Since discipline, sacrifice and related concepts are neither good nor bad as such, their meaning should not be decided theoretically once and for all, but rather, an empiricist would claim, be assessed on a case-to-case basis.

Both exponents of nationalism say violence within "our" religion is only "in the name of" it, while creeds we oppose are violence at heart. Political ideologies and religion rely on similar ideas – other-worldly existence, and a thousand-year-empire called Millennialism – but religions are still "innately peaceful." The scientist would reply religions are man-made and not infallible – which, of course, leaves very little left of religion. The emotional rhetoric of religious backers testifies, if anything, to their disadvantage. In general, religion fuels violent sentiments.[3] According to Census Bureau Data, professed atheists among prisoners in the United States in 2008 is 0.1 per cent, while 8.4 per cent are Muslims. If we take the proportion of each group into account – 0.7 per cent versus 0.6 per cent – the likelihood of any one Muslim to be in jail is about 100 times higher compared to an atheist. This seems to indicate that atheism fosters a less violent lifestyle as compared to religion in case Islam can be taken as an example.[4] If terrorists cite its holy books, it is likely to mean something. We ought, George Orwell maintains, to listen to what people say instead of clinging to exotifying assumptions about their clean, honourable motives. Suggesting "we" know what "they" really mean is an elitist, anti-liberal 'assumption.

These two manifestations of nationalism are two branches of the romantic tree going back to the counter-Enlightenment of the early 19th-century. All those traits of relativism prevalent in positive nationalism – ethnic haughtiness, collectivism, or language mysticism – recur in masochist nationalism. In order to break with positive nationalism, we must not merely swing from one conceited romanticism over to another but discard the very ideas of romanticism and lazy relativism for the benefit of cautious universalism and a quest for similarities. We have the right to regard others are beasts, while they should feel free to consider us as brutes. A liberal would insist on self-determination, not only for "us" but everywhere as a principle.

Positive and masochist nationalists share body language and gestures. While one put his head up and his voice down to instil a sense of hierarchy, the other puts his voice up and his head down to deny cultural privileges. None of them pay attention to the fact that they are actually standing in front of human beings who might have something to say. It is all prefabricated and patronising, whether from above of from below. Only show interest, a humanist would suggest, when people are interesting. Don't get caught in your intellectual assumptions or utopianism, but observe the world as it is, and acknowledge that starvation is not a potential for something else but starvation accomplished.

With little compassion, positive nationalists keep bringing up the poor's lack of hygiene, while masochist nationalists, at times with an unclear laughter, tend to avoid the topic altogether. They both fail to understand the stifling impact of social circumstances, instead believing poverty rests on free will to be either

126 Liberal way out of nationalist ossification

adored or despised. Either way, the poor are caught in their destitution. Instead, as liberals or classic socialists, we ought to keep addressing lack of hygiene as a call for social improvement. People are never inhuman, but their situation might be. If socialist academics back then had believed their bathroom would constitute an abuse in the eyes of mid-England miners, there might never have been any improvement of living conditions at all. Whether you have bought into the illusions of distance or the illusions of intimacy, your gestures and attitudes are equally condescending. Here, George Orwell might offer a way out. Avoid any false intimacy. Dirt is never a choice. Acknowledge your privileges but remember that these privileges are basically the product of good fortune and that they one day will have to go.

Conclusively, a few words about those racist tendencies in either form of nationalism and how to escape them. White race is superior, positive nationalists say, while masochist nationalists say the black race is the peak of creation. When you meet someone regardless of skin complexion, a liberal might suggest, you will benefit from their knowledge, or they will profit from your insights. There is no competition, and nothing to be worried about. The Swedish author August Strindberg illustrates this generous and eager attitude. His conversations with a good friend in Paris, he says, were amazing "feasts of love" and "we parted trembling, not knowing what was yours and mine, looking at those creations of our common fantasy, these thoughts with two fathers behind them."[5]

Skin colour is a racist categorization whether you push for whites or for people of colour. Martin Luther King's intellectualist plea for a "colour blind society" stands in stark contrast to this. Physiognomy is a racist mode of selection whether you find a particular cheekbone intriguing or disqualifying. Rather than studying their face, we could listen to what people say. Obsession by the colourful or the uniform signifies a superficial attitude. Instead, we could bring out the individual in all her complexity. "Blacks only!" is only "Whites only!" from the other end. Either way, we are reduced to silent exhibitionists displaying our ethnic exterior. Instead of this pessimistic racial segregation, the liberal way out leads to modest optimism and a quest for commonalities and shared interests – if possible. We should stay away from racist slurs in either direction – whether "nigger" of "white-trash." A black homeless person in Mombasa and a white person in an Oklahoma trailer-park are both worthy of our compassion.

An individualist society is reflected by solidarity throughout the electorate. Supporters of one's opponents should be treated with respect hoping you might one day win them over. When voters are dehumanised by positive nationalists or masochist nationalists, as Hillary Clinton did recently, she is giving up on ever regaining their votes. True to this idea, she also calls them "irredeemable."[6] In addition, the electorate is further polarised by the fact that her breach of a political code of conduct will further radicalise and brutalise her own backers. Clinton's carelessness also suggests that political power may no longer rest on voter support. The way out, then, would be to cater for the entire electorate and prevent liberal mainstream from caving in.

Anyone to the left of the far-right, some positive nationalists say, is a revolutionary undermining society, and anyone questioning the orthodoxy of identity politics, says masochist nationalists, is a racist, or even Fascist. Instead of polarising the political spectrum, a social democrat or liberal would suggest, we should endeavour to create broad democratic alliances against extremists on either side. Ideological stereotyping should be avoided, because we are never "fascinated" by an individual. Fascination implies intolerance. A society shows democratic maturity when individuals are not put on a pedestal for scorn or admiration but freely walk around among us. Instead of masochist nationalist kitschy images of far-off cultures, we must, a liberal would insist, ensure that these images are authentic, displaying overseas' cultures in all their impenetrable complexity. Otherwise these images will gradually fuse with commercial messages, and blend with positive nationalists' close ties with neo-liberalism along with their colonial, superficial gaze at countries on the other side of the horizon.

Notes

1 Mill, 2015, p. 117.
2 Popper, 2011, pp. 159-68.
3 Adamson, 2011.
4 "Are Prisoners Less Likely To Be Atheists?," 2015.
5 Lagerkrantz, 1979, p. 128.
6 "Hillary Clinton Calls Many Trump Backers 'Deplorables,' and G.O.P. Pounces," 10 September, 2016.

13

A FINAL WORD

This book is about a political similarity. The nationalist has a lot in common with his most fearsome critic. Not on the surface, of course. On the face of it, they are saying very different things, perhaps even opposite things. But if you look at the principles they are fighting for instead of the geographical setting where these principles come to life, it is hard to tell one from the other.

The positive nationalists: Trump, Brexiteers, Victor Orbán, *Sweden Democrats*, *Alternative für Deutschland*, Marine Le Pen's *Front National*, the Greek *Golden Dawn* and other ultra-right-wingers in Eastern Europe. The masochist nationalists: The entourage of the UN and the EU, the Clintons and the Washington elites, *New York Times* and *The Guardian*, the universities, the multiculturalists, the politically correct, and the left-wing establishment. Today's political discussion is practically defined by this conflict. It all started in an essay by George Orwell, where he sensationally suggested that the major political disagreement of our time boils down to one piece of turf traded for another. You are standing over there, and we are standing over here, and that's all there is. If Orwell's insight was to become public knowledge, the political debate in the West would perhaps have to be reconsidered altogether.

REFERENCES

20020118 – Gudrun Schyman: "Talibantalet", tal på Vänsterpartiets kongress 2002, 18 January, 2002. http://www.svenskatal.se/20020118-gudrun-schyman-talibantalet-tal-pa-vansterpartiets-kongress-2002/, Accessed 26 April, 2020.

80 per cent agree Lord's Prayer SHOULD be screened at cinemas as Richard Dawkins backs ad, *Express*, Nov 23, 2015. https://www.express.co.uk/news/uk/621437/Express-poll-results-show-four-five-think-Lord-s-Prayer-should-be-shown. Accessed 24 April, 2020.

Adbel-Samad, Hamed, *Der Untergang der Islamischen Welt – Eine Prognose* (Munich: Knaur, 2010).

Adamson, Göran, Atheism, in Jeffrey Ian Ross (ed.), *Religion and Violence: An Encyclopedia of Faith and Conflict from Antiquity to the Present* (London: Routledge, 2011).

Adamson, Göran, "Migrants and Crime in Sweden in the 21st Century (*Society*, Jan/Feb, 2020)

Adamson, Göran, "Education in Sweden: Then Things Got Interesting" (Gatestone Institute, 2016a). https://www.gatestoneinstitute.org/9600/sweden-education, Accessed 28 April, 2020.

Adamson, Göran, *Populists Parties and the Failure of the Political Elites – The Rise of the Austrian Freedom Party (FPÖ)* (Frankfurt/M: Peter Lang, 2016b).

Adolf Hitler – Mångfaldens fiende. Öppen föreläsning, *Malmö Högskola*, 20 Oct, 2010. http://www.mah.se/Nyheter/Nyheter-2010/Adolf-Hitler--mangfaldens-fiende/. Accessed 24 April, 2010.

Ambassador: Cancel provocative Roma art exhibit. 9 October, 2013. https://bbj.hu/politics/ambassador-cancel-provocative-roma-art-exhibit_70367, Accessed 24 April, 2020.

"Are Prisoners Less Likely To Be Atheists?", *ABC News*, 12 March, 2015), https://fivethirtyeight.com/features/are-prisoners-less-likely-to-be-atheists/, Accessed 28 April, 2020.

Artleaks, Hungarian Ambassador intervenes Against "anti-Hungarian" Art Exhibition in Linz, 3 October, 2013, https://art-leaks.org/2013/10/03/hungarian-ambassador-intervenes-against-anti-hungarian-art-exhibition-in-linz/, Accessed 24 April, 2020

Asante, Molefe Kete, *Afrocentricity* (Trenton: African World Press, 1988).

Asande, Molefi Kete, An Afrocentric Curriculum, *Educational Leadership* 49(4) (December 1991–January 1992).

130 References

Ashura Day 2016: Marble Arch and Oxford Street traffic stands still as Muslims march on holy day, Evening Standard, 12 October, 2016).

Ayaan Hirsi Ali on the West, Dawa and Islam, *Hoover Institution*, Interview, *Peter Robinson* https://www.youtube.com/watch?v=Bx2hEc7Dlcg&t=320s, Accessed 26 April, 2020.

Ban art that targets far right, says Hungarian ambassador, http://www.indexoncensorship.org/2013/10/ban-art-targets-far-right-says-hungarian-ambassador/, Accessed 24 April, 2020.

Banner-Haley, C.P, We Can't Go Home Again: An Argument about Afrocentrism, *Journal of Southern History* 69(3) (2003), pp. 663–665.

Berlingske Tidene, 19 feb, 2005

"Bildt: Det har spridits bekymmersamma bilder av Sverige", 18 jan, 2017. http://www.aftonbladet.se/nyheter/samhalle/a/7zRpK/bildt-det-har-spridits-bekymmersamma-bilder-av-sverige, Accessed 26 April, 2020.

Lawrence, *I'm Not a Racist, … But – The Moral Quandary of Race* (Ithaca, NY: Cornell UP, 2002).

Du Bois, W. E. B., The Conservation of Races, in *On Sociology and the Black Community*, Dan S. Green, and Edwin D. Driver (eds.) (Chicago: University of Chicago Press, 1978).

Du Bois, W. E. B., *The Souls of Black Folk* (Oxford: Oxford University Press, 2007).

Bawer, Bruce, *While Europe Slept – How Radical Islam Is Destroying the West from Within* (New York: Doubleday, 2006).

Berlin, Isaiah, Herder and the Enlightenment, in *The Proper Study of Mankind: An Anthology of Ideas* Henry Hardy and Roger Hausheer (eds.) (London: Pimlico, 1998).

Bollywood has denigrated women, says Victor Banerjee, *The Times of India,* 6 March, 2013, http://timesofindia.indiatimes.com/entertainment/hindi/bollywood/news/Bollywood-has-denigrated-women-says-Victor-Banerjee/articleshow/18811907.cms, Accessed 24 April, 2020.

"BRÅ: Kvinnors Otrygghet alarmerande". http://www.sydsvenskan.se/2017-01-10/bra-kvinnors-otrygghet-alarmerande, Accessed 24 April, 2020

Brea, Johanni, Urbanczik, Robert, and Senn, Walter, "A Normative Theory of Forgetting: Lessons from the Fruit Fly", Jean Daunizeau (ed.), *Computational Biology* (June 5, 2014)

"Brown sauce sales are falling: has Britain finally come to its senses?", The Guardian, 5 Jan, 2015.

Bruckner, Pascal, *The Tyranny of Guilt – An Essay on Western Masochism* (Princeton: Princeton University Press, 2010).

Caldwell, Christopher, *Reflections on the Revolution in Europe: Immigration, Islam and the West* (New York: Anchor Books, 2010).

Conversation with Park (Facebook, Messenger, 25 April, 2020).

Daiva, K. Stasiulis, Participation by Immigrants, Ethnocultural/visible Minorities in the Canadian Political Process, in Participation by Immigrants, Ethnocultural/visible Minorities in the Canadian Political Process Göran Adamson (ed.), *Immigrants and Political Participation – Background, Theory, and Empirical Suggestions* (Vienna: European Union Monitoring Centre on Racism and Xenophobia, 2002).

Dan Parks forbudte billeder vises på Christiansborg i dag, 23 Oct, 2014. https://politiken.dk/kultur/kunst/art5549260/Dan-Parks-forbudte-billeder-vises-p%C3%A5-Christiansborg-i-dag, Accessed 24 April, 2020

Dan Park till åklagaren: Det är ju ni som har svarta på hjärnan!, *Ingrid och Maria* (3 April, 2019) https://www.ingridochmaria.se/2019/04/03/dan-park-till-aklagaren-det-ar-ju-ni-som-har-svarta-pa-hjarnan/, Accessed 24 April, 2020

"Därför äter vi svenskar så konstig mat", SvT, Nyheter, Inrikes, 30 June, 2018. https://www.svt.se/nyheter/inrikes/darfor-ater-vi-svenskar-sa-konstig-mat. Accessed 24 April, 2020

Diop, Cheikh Anta, *The African Origin of Civilization: Myth or Reality* (Chicago, Illinois: Lawrence Hill Books, 1974).

Edlund, Helena, *Konsten Att överleva Svenska Kyrkan* (Stockholm: *Vulkan*, 2018).

References **131**

Einsatzleiger rechnete "nicht anssatzweise" mit Köln-Exzessen, 18 March, 2016. https://www.morgenpost.de/vermischtes/article207222327/Einsatzleiter-rechnete-nicht-ansatzweise-mit-Koeln-Exzessen.html, 26 April, 2020

Elisabeth Höglund, "Lars Vilks missbrukar yttrandefriheten", 25 Feb, 2013. https://www.aftonbladet.se/nyheter/kolumnister/a/a230GO/lars-vilks-missbrukar-yttrandefriheten. Accessed 24 April, 2020

Email to all residents at The Natural Park, Sukhumvit Soi 49, Bangkok (May 29, 2016.)

Eriksen, Jens Martin & Stjernfelt, Frederik, *Adskillelsens Politik: Multikulturalisme – Ideologi Og Virkelighed* (Köpenhamn: Lindhardt og Ringhof, 2008).

"Fängsla konstnärer som målar könsorgan", 17 June, 2014. http://www.svt.se/kultur/fangsla-konstnarer-som-malar-konsorgan, Accessed 24 April, 2020

"Feministiskt initiativ: Svenska män kan vara värst i världen på trakasserier och våld mot kvinnor", https://jamstalldhetsfeministern.wordpress.com/2016/01/09/feministiskt-in-itiativ-svenska-man-kan-vara-varst-i-varlden-pa-massattacker-mot-kvinnor/, Accessed 26 April, 2020

Fourest, Caroline, *La Tentasion Obscurantiste* (Paris: Grasset, 2005).

Frankell, Eva, "Löfven tar över ett skitigt land" (Aftonbladet, 30 Sept, 2014)

Fraser, Nancy, "From Redistribution to Recognition? Dilemmas of Justice in a "Post-Socialist" Age" (*New Left Review*, 1995)

Friedman, Jonathan," Cosmopolitan Elites, Organic Intellectuals and the Re-Configuration of the State", Kouvouama, Abel et al (eds.) *Figures croisées d'intellectuels. Trajectoires, Modes d'action, Productions* (Paris: Karthala, 2007)

Galtung, Johan, "On the Effects of International Economic Sanctions: With Examples from the Case of Rhodesia" (World Politics, 1 April, 1967, Vol. 19(3)

"Gatukonstnären Dan Park döms till fängelse - för hets mot folkgrupp" (SvT, 8 Nov. 2018). https://www.svt.se/kultur/gatukonstnaren-dan-park-doms-till-fangelse-for-hets-mot-folkgrupp, Accessed 24 April, 2020

Gedicht über Erdogan: Merkel räumt Fehler in Böhmermann-Affäre ein, 22 April 2016. http://www.spiegel.de/politik/deutschland/jan-boehmermann-angela-merkel-raeumt-fehler-ein-a-1088861.html, Accessed 26 April, 2020

Goldstein, Robert Justin, *Censorship of Political Caricature in Nineteenth-Century France* (Kent, OH: Kent State University Press, 1989).

Goodhart, David, *The Road to Somewhere - The New Tribes Shaping British Politics* (London: Penguin, 2017).

Henry Bosnu, "My life in media, *The Independent Online,* 11 Sept., 2006. http://www.independent.co.uk/news/media/henry-bonsu-my-life-in-media-415461.html. Accessed 24 April, 2020

Herder, Johann Gottfried, *Herders Sämmtliche Werke,* Bernhard Suphan, (ed.) (Berlin: Weidmann, 1877–1913)

"Hillary Clinton Calls Many Trump Backers 'Deplorables,' and G.O.P. Pounces", Sept. 10, 2016. http://www.nytimes.com/2016/09/11/us/politics/hillary-clinton-basket-of-deplorables.html?_r=0, Accessed 26 April, 2020

Hillary Clinton on Twitter, 19 Nov, 2015. https://twitter.com/hillaryclinton/status/667371059885301761, Accessed 26 April, 2020

Hirsi Ali, Ayaan, *Infidel* (New York: FREE PRESS, 2008).

Hirsi Ali, Ayaan, *Nomad. From Islam to America: A Personal Journey Through the Clash of Civilizations* (New York: FREE PRESS, 2010).

"*Ignore Vilks' Muhammad show: religious heads". (The Local*, 26 Feb, 2013). https://www.thelocal.se/20130226/46416, Accessed 24 April, 2020

"Im Geist des Eroberers" (*Süddeutsche Zeitung,* 28 July, 2020)

132 References

"Inledande bestämmelser", *Diskrimineringslagen* (Kapitel 1, 5 §, "Kön könsöverskridande identitet eller uttryck, etnisk tillhörighet, funktionshinder, sexuell läggning och ålder", 3. "Etnisk tillhörighet"). http://www.notisum.se/rnp/sls/lag/20080567.htm, Accessed 28 April, 2020

Iran Human Rights Documentation Center, Murder at Mykonos: Anatomy of a Political Assassination. http://www.iranhrdc.org/english/publications/reports/3150-murder-at-mykonos-anatomy-of-a-political-assassination.html. ACeesse 24 April, 2020

Jewish Life in the Americas, 23 Sept, 2008. https://lifeandletters.la.utexas.edu/2008/09/jewish-life-in-the-americas/, Accessed 15 May, 2020

Karl Marx, Suppression of the *Neue Rheinische Zeitung, Neue Rheinische Zeitung* (No. 301, May 1849) https://www.marxists.org/archive/marx/works/1849/05/19c.htm#terror, Accessed 26 April, 2020

Kenan Malik, "Against Multiculturalism" (*New Humanist*, 31 May, 2007) https://newhumanist.org.uk/articles/523/against-multiculturalism, Accessed 24 April, 2020

Malik, Kenan, *debates – can multiculturalism work?* http://www.kenanmalik.com/lectures/multiculturalism_if.html, Accessed 29 April, 2020

Kirfel, Martina, and Walter Oswalt (eds.), *Die Rückkehr der Führer - Modernisierter Rechtsradikalismus in Westeuropa* (Vienna: Europaverlag, 1989).

"Kölner Silvester-Angriffe: 1075 Anzeigen und 73 Verdächtige". Der Westen Funke NRW. 16 Feb, 2016 https://www.derwesten.de/politik/koelner-silvester-angriffe-1075-anzeigen-und-73-verdaechtige-id11567004.html

Kowalsky, Wolfgang, *Rechtsaussen… und die verfehlten Strategien der Deutschen Linken* (Frankfurt/M: Ullstein, 1992).

Kristoffer Larsson, "Something is rotten in Sweden", The Translators Network for Linguistic Diversity, 20 Oct, 2007. http://www.tlaxcala.es/pp.asp?lg=en&reference=3949, Accessed 24 April, 2020

Kumar, Vijaya, *The World's Greatest Speeches* (India: New Dawn Press, 2006).

Lagerkrantz, Olof, *August Strindberg* (Stockholm: Wahlström & Widstrand, 1979).

"Lars Vilks, Gay Mohammed and Freedom of Expression" (*The American Catholic*, 16 May, 2010). https://www.the-american-catholic.com/2010/05/16/lars-vilks-gay-muhammad-and-freedom-of-expression/, Accessed 24 April, 2020

"Lars Vilks Rondellhundar: Ett förlöjligande utan syfte" (Skånska Dagbladet, 14 June, 2010), https://www.skd.se/2010/06/14/lars-vilks-rondellhundar-ett-forlojligande-utan-syfte/, Accessed 24 April, 2020

Leavitt, Byron, *The Complete Cancer Diaries: One Man's Journey Into Darkness, Wonder and Hope* (Tacoma: Brainwaves Press, 2015).

Ledare: Kärnvärdena gäller alla (SDS, 10 Feb, 2010) https://www.sydsvenskan.se/2010-02-09/karnvardena-galler-alla, Accessed 24 April, 2020

Lenk, Kurt, *Rechts, Wo Die Mitte Ist, Studien Zur Ideologie: Rechtsextremismus, Nationalsozialismus, Konservatismus* (Nomos: Baden-Baden, 1994).

Lombroso, Cesare, *Criminal Man - According to the Classification of Cesare Lombroso* (New York: G. P Putnam's Sons, 1911).

Malik, Kenan, "Making a Difference: Culture, race and social policy" (Patterns of Prejudice, Vol. 39, Issue 4, Dec 2005)

Malik, Kenan, "Can Multiculturalism Work?" at *Attention Seeking: Multiculturalism and the Politics of Recognition* (London: Institute français, 2002), CanMultiCultWork(1).pdf

Médecins Sans Frontières is 'institutionally racist', say 1,000 insiders (*the Guardian*, 10 July, 2020)

"Mehr als 1500 Straftaten: Die Ermittlungsergebnisse zur Kölner Silvesternacht". *Der Spiegel* 6 April, 2016. https://www.spiegel.de/panorama/justiz/koeln-silvesteruebergriffe-die-ermittlungsergebnisse-a-1085716.html

References **133**

Mill, J.S., *On Liberty* (London: Broadview Edition, 2015).

Mills, Stephanie, *Turning Away from Technology: A New Vision for the 21st Century* (New Catalyst Books, 1997)

Minogue, Kenneth, Introduction - Multiculturalism: A Dictatorship of Virtue, in Introduction - Multiculturalism: A Dictatorship of Virtue Patrick West (ed.), *The Poverty of Multiculturalism* (London: Civitas, 2005).

'Mona Sahlin: Sverigedemokraternas bästa vän!' http://ligator.wordpress.com/2010/08/14/mona-sahlin-sverigedemokraternas-basta-van/. Accessed 24 April, 2020

"Mördarens val av offer: "De såg svenska ut." (Västmanlandläns tidning, 21 Oct, 2015)

Mehmet Ümit Necef, *ETNISK KITSCH - og andre (post)moderne fortaellingar om "de andre"* (Köpenhavn: Köpenhavns Universitet, 1994).

"Om Diskrimineringsombudsmannen". http://www.do.se/om-diskriminering/skyddade-diskrimineringsgrunder/, Accessed 24 April, 2020

Orwell, George, *Notes on Nationalism* (London: Polemic, 1945).

Orwell, George, *The Road to Wigan Pier* (London: *Penguin Classics*, 2001).

Parekh, Bhikhu, *Rethinking Multiculturalism, Cultural Diversity and Political Theory* (Basingstoke: Macmillan, 2000).

Parfit, Derek, *Reasons and Persons* (Oxford: Oxford University Press, 1984).

Pape, R. A., Why Economic Sanctions Do Not Work, *International Security* 22(2) (1997).

Pfahl-Traughber, Armin, Brücken Zwischen Rechtsextremismus und Konservativismus - Zur Erosion der Abgrenzung auf Publizistischer Ebene in den achtziger und Neunziger Jahren", in Wolfgang Kowalsky, and Wolfgang Schroeder (eds.), *Rechtsextremismus - Einführung und Forschungsbilanz* (Opladen: Westdeutscher Verlag, 1994).

Parekh, Bhikhu, *Rethinking Multiculturalism, Cultural Diversity and Political Theory*, (Basingstoke: Macmillan, 2000), p. 68.

Phillips, Anne, *The Politics of Presence* (Oxford: Clarendon Press, 1995).

"Peter Weiderud: Dags att ta avstånd från Vilks hädelser" (*Expressen*, 14 dec, 2010).

"Praise Allah" bus slogans get green light just months after Lord's Prayer ad gets banned. http://www.express.co.uk/news/uk/668398/Praise-Allah-bus-slogans-get-green-light-just-months-after-Lord-s-Prayer-ad-gets-banned. Accessed 24 April, 2020

"Polisen: Offer väljs ut för att de är svenskar. https://www.sydsvenskan.se/2016-03-13/polisen-offer-valjs-ut-for-att-de-ar-svenskar, Accessed 24 April, 2020

Polizisten machen widersprüchliche Aussagen zu Kölner Silvesternacht, Süddeutsche Zeitung 18 March 2016 https://www.sueddeutsche.de/panorama/untersuchungsausschuss-polizisten-machen-widerspruechliche-aussagen-zu-koelner-silvesternacht-1.2914635, Accessed 26 April, 2020

Popper, Karl, *The Open Society and Its Enemies* (London: Routledge, 2011, Vol. 1)

Ravitch, Diane, Multiculturalism: E Pluribus Plures, *American Scholar* 59(3) (1990).

Richards, Blake A, and Paul W. Frankland, The Persistence and Transience of Memory, *Neuron* ((June 21, 2017).

Robert Stasinski - "Fallet Dan Park", Konstnärernas Riksorganisation, 2014. http://www.kro.se/konstnaren_3_2014_fallet_dan_parks, Accessed 24 April, 2020

Sentenced: Swedish Artist Dan Park "Incited Against an Ethnic Group", 12 Oct, 2014, https://hyperallergic.com/154676/sentenced-swedish-artist-dan-park-incited-against-an-ethnic-group/, Accessed 24 April, 2020

Silvesternacht in Köln: Offenbar viel weniger Polizisten im Einsatz als gedacht. Süddeutsche Zeitung https://www.sueddeutsche.de/panorama/nach-den-uebergriffen-in-koeln-silvesternac-ht-in-koeln-offenbar-waren-viel-weniger-polizisten-im-einsatz-als-gedacht-1.2911408, 17 March, 2016

Sabbage, Sophie, *The Cancer Whisperer - How to Let Cancer Heal Your Life* (London: Coronet, 2016).

134 References

SAS - "What is truly Scandinavian?", https://www.youtube.com/watch?v=ShfsBPrNcTI, Accessed 14 June, 2020

Stern, Fritz, *The Politics of Cultural Despair* (Berkeley: University of California Press, 1974).

Statements by François Hollande, President of the Republic: 9 Jan. 2015. http://www.consulfrance-losangeles.org/spip.php?article2554, Accessed 26 April, 2020

Swedish artist jailed for "race hate" pictures (21 Aug, 2014). https://www.thelocal.se/20140821/swedish-artist-jailed-for-race-hate-pictures, Accessed 24 April, 2020

Tät gemenskap både välsignelse och förbannelse, 21 Jan, 2004. http://www.svd.se/nyheter/idagsidan/existentiellt/tat-gemenskap-bade-valsignelse-och-forbannelse_125297.svd#,

Taylor, Charles, "The Importance of Herder," in *Philosophical Arguments* (Cambridge, MA: Harvard University Press, 1997)

Text: President Bush Addresses the Nation, *The Washington Post,* September 20, 2001, https://www.washingtonpost.com/wp-srv/nation/specials/attacked/transcripts/bushaddress_092001.html, Accessed 27 April, 2020

The Afrocentric education crisis. http://prospect.org/article/afrocentric-education-crisis. 27 April, 2020

The Global Gender Gap Report 2018. https://www.weforum.org/reports/the-global-gender-gap-report-2018, Accessed 13 Aug, 2020

This is how to get more girls into school in Afghanistan https://www.weforum.org/agenda/2016/03/what-does-the-future-hold-for-afghanistan/ Accessed 13 Aug, 2020

"Tio minnesvärda citat av Reinfeldt", *Svenska Dagbladet*, Oct. 9, 2014.

Totten, Samuel, "Chronology: The Darfur Crisis", in Samuel Totten, Eric Markusen (ed.). *Genocide in Darfur: Investigating the Atrocities in the Sudan* (London: Routledge, 2006)

Townsend, Peter, *Nothing to Do With Islam? Investigating the World's Most Dangerous Blind Spot(Createspace Independence*, 2016).

"Två partiledare ger Vilks del av skulden", (SDS, 19 maj, 2010.) https://www.sydsvenskan.se/2010-05-19/tva-partiledare-ger-vilks-del-av-skulden. Accessed 24 April, 2020

"Vikten av att vara Vilks" (SvD, 27 juni 2010)

"Vilks kan ju inte rita" (*Aftonbladet*, 15 mars 2010)

Vohra, Ranbir, *The Making of India: A Historical Survey* (New York: M. E. Sharpe, 2001).

Wallensteen, Peter, *Ekonomiska Sanktioner* (Halmstad: Prisma, 1971).

Webster, Yehudi O., *Against the Multicultural Agenda - A Critical Thinking Alternative* (Westport: Connecticut & London: Praeger, 1997).

West, Patrick, *The Poverty of Multiculturalism* (London: Civitas, 2005).

'When I was diagnosed with terminal cancer the first thing on my bucket list was to leave my husband', *Daily Mirror*, 13 May, 2017

Wikipedia: Sara Svensson. http://others.sensagent.com/sara+svensson/sv-sv/, Accessed 26 April, 2020

Wolin, Richard, Designer Fascism, in Designer FascismRichard J. Golsan (ed.), *Fascism's Return: Scandal, Revision, and Ideology Since 1980* (Lincoln: University of Nebraska Press, 1998).

INDEX

Note: Page numbers followed by 'n' refer to notes.

absolutism 19
Adamson, Göran 86
Addis Ababa 75, 93, 114
aestheticization, of violence 80
Afghanistan 55, 73, 74
Afrocentricity 24–25, 109
Alternative für Deutschland 128
altruism 72, 75
amnesia, virtue of 27–37
Anarchical and Revolutionary Crimes
    Act of 1919 53
Andersson, Benedict 105
Anglophobia 3, 4
antagonism 6
anti-intellectualism 90
anti-racism 19
Arendt, Hannah 35
art 6, 38–45, 82, 122
artistic freedom 6, 38–42, 44, 45, 79, 122
artistic rebellion 42–44, 122
Asante, Molefi 109

bad forgetting problem 27–29
Banerjee, Victor 12
Banner-Haley, C.P. 24
Bawer, Bruce 28, 60, 107
Berger, Peter 20
Bergh, Lise 9
Berlin, Isaiah 91
Black Lives Matter 117
Blair, Tony 85, 86

Blum, Lawrence 88
Bobrovniczky, Vince Szalay 38, 39
Böhmermann, Jan 78, 79
Bollywood 12
Bone, Pamela 73
Brea, Johanni 28
British Tory 3
Bromwich, David 50
Bruckner, Pascal 28
Bush, George 85

Caldwell, Christopher 13, 21, 78
Chekov, Anton 57, 58
The Cherry Orchard 57
Church of Philadelphia 84
Clinton, Hillary 85, 126
cognitive dissonance 12
collectivism, ogre of 47–56; ethnic dis-
    crimination, mystifying 49–53; foreign
    intrusion 53–56; inequality 47–49
colour-blind society 114
condescension, gestures of 92–98
conflicts 17
The Conservation of Races 88
Counter-Enlightenment 87, 100, 125
crime rate 63–65, 67
Criminal Man 105
cult of death 6, 77–83, 124
cult of power 61
cult of powerlessness 61
cult of violence 62

136 Index

cultural differences 36, 96
culturalism 89
cultural prejudices 96
cultural recognition 36, 124
cultures 8, 11–13, 22, 24, 30, 32, 47, 53,
  75, 87–89, 91, 92, 100, 116, 120, 121

Dahl, Thulesen 82
death cult 6, 77–83, 124
de Maistre, Joseph 80
democracy 9, 17, 19, 86, 115, 116
democratic maturity 113, 115–116, 127
Der Mensch und die Technik 81
discrimination 1, 49–53, 74, 100, 104,
  114, 122
Diskrimineringsombudsmannen (DO)
  49–51
Dostoevsky 86
Du Bois, W. E. B. 88
Dutch politics 5

emotions 57–62
equality 35, 36, 47, 122
Erdogan, Recip 78, 79
ethnic belonging 104
ethnic discrimination 52, 122; mystifying
  49–53
ethnic kitsch 20
ethnic self-importance 121
ethnocentric history books 23–25
ethno-pluralism 88, 109
European colonialism 52
European ethnocentricity 24
Euroturk 9
exotic cultures 5, 9, 11, 88, 89, 105, 107,
  115, 116, 118, 120, 122, 123

fascination 5, 11, 81, 93, 107, 109,
  113–115, 127
fascism 17, 19, 33, 59, 82, 90, 100, 103,
  120, 121
Female Genital Mutilation (FGM) 107
Fischer, Heinz 38
foreign intrusion 47, 53–56, 90, 123
Frankland, Paul W. 28
Fraser, Nancy 36
Front National 128

Galtung, Johan 55
"Gargantua" 58
Gellner, Ernest 105
gender stereotypes 12
generosity, lack of 72–75
German identity 32, 33
Gollancz, Victor 94

Goodhart, David 6, 34
Gosenius, Susanne 48
Greek Golden Dawn 8, 29, 32, 128
Greer, Germaine 73–75
group fanaticism 27, 29–34, 121
group mysticism 30
Guillou, Jan 43

Habermas, Jürgen 17
Haider, Jörg 54, 55
hate crime 47–48, 122
Havel, Vaclav 83n1
Herder, Johann Gottfried 87–92
Hirsi Ali, Ayaan 30, 53
historical kitsch 20–23, 78, 121
Hitler, Adolf 35, 38
Hoggart, Richard 94
Hollande, Francois 85
home-language education 10
humour 77–80, 124
Husayn, Imam 28

identity 32
identity politics 33
ideological stereotyping 112–117
Ideomeneo 79
inequality 47–49
injustice 1, 28–29, 122

Jespersen, Karen 9
Jyllands-Posten 58, 79

King, Martin Luther 107, 108, 126
kitsch, historical 20–23, 78, 121
knowledge 13, 14, 60–62, 103, 114, 115,
  121, 123, 126
Kowalsky, Wolfgang 9, 33, 34

Larsson, Margareta 38, 39
Law against Discrimination 104
leadership 80
Le Pen, Jean-Marie 109
lethargy 18
Linna, Katri 51
Linz exhibition 41, 45
Löfven, Stefan 10, 48
Lombroso, Cesare 105, 106

majestic poetry, misapprehensions 16–20
Malik, Kenan 35, 50
Malmö University College 8
Malraux, André 18
Mannheim, Karl 77
Marx, Karl 60
masochist nationalist difference 35

Index **137**

Mbuti society 20
memory 121
meritocracy 123
Merkel, Angela 78, 79
Michaloliakos, Nikolaos 8, 29
Michel, Louis 55
Mill, J. S. 123, 124
Minogue, Kenneth 7n5
moral show-off 63–76
Mugabe, Robert 30
Muhammad cartoons 79
Müller, Adam 29
multicultural exoticism 9
multiculturalism 32, 35, 88, 91, 103
multicultural self-esteem 91
Muslims 15, 27, 58, 59, 69, 85, 102, 125

Nasrin, Taslima 119n22
nationalism 1, 2n1, 8, 61, 90, 120, 121;
    see also individual entries
nationalist ossification 120–127
National Socialism 38–40, 61, 71, 81, 86,
    122
Nazis 111–112
Necef, Mehmet Ümit 20
negative nationalism 3–4, 65
neo-liberalism 117–118, 127
Nerikes Allehanda 39
Neue Rheinische Zeitung 60
Nietzsche, Friedrich 112
niggers 110–111
Notes on nationalism 3, 4
Nothing to do with Islam? 85

obsession 3, 11, 28, 34, 51, 79, 100, 101,
    106, 107, 121, 126; colourful 107–108;
    with difference 34–36
Ohly, Lars 39, 40, 42, 44
One America News Network (OANN) 77
one romantic tree, two branches 87–92
Orwell, George 2n1, 3, 4, 6, 11, 13, 19,
    21, 23, 25, 43, 49, 54, 55, 73, 80, 82,
    94–98, 106, 114, 115, 125, 126, 128

Parekh, Bhikhu 88
Park, Dan 39, 40, 43–45
Pasolini, Paolo 80
patriotism 2n1
pessimism 17, 63–72, 123
Phillips, Anne 31
physiognomy 101, 105–107, 110,
    126
political art 38, 39, 41–42, 122
political exceptionalism 17
political rule of thumb 58

The Politics of Cultural Despair 90
Popper, Karl 124
positive nationalism 8, 22, 23, 29, 35, 53,
    61, 72, 101, 110
power 57–62; of culture 10–16; of roots
    8–10
powerlessness 60–61, 123
primitivism 14

racial hierarchies 100–104, 116
racial inventory 106
racism 36, 100–119; ideological
    stereotyping 112–117; Nazis and
    revolutionaries 111–112; obsession
    by colourful 107–108; physiognomy
    105–107; racial hierarchies 101–104;
    racist name-calling, niggers and white
    trash 110–111; skin colour 104–105;
    unfair allegations 111–112; viru-
    lent nationalism and neo-liberalism
    117–118; whites only! blacks only!
    108–110
racist name-calling 110–111
Rasmussen, Linda 45
Ravitch, Diane 25
reactionary onslaught on wit 77–80
Reinfeldt, Fredrik 9
religious violence 84–86
revolutionaries 111–112
Richards, Blake A. 28
Rite of Spring 43
*The Road to Somewhere – The New Tribes
    Shaping British Politics* 6
The Road to Wigan Pier 95, 114
Rowlatt Act 53

Sahlin, Mona 9
Schyman, Gudrun 73–75
scientific racism 106
self-abasement 29, 63–76
self-accusation 1
self-aggrandisement 1
self-annihilation 82
self-critical nationalism 2, 4
self-defeatism 19, 78
self-determination 3, 32
self-flagellation 29
self-obsession 18
self-reflection 10, 77, 79–80
self-righteous nationalism 1
skin colour 100, 104–107, 109, 110, 118,
    126
Smith, Anthony 105
Snoilsky, Carl 16–18, 20
Sob, Brigitte 81

138 Index

Solzhenitsyn, Alexander 60
The Souls of Black Folk 88
Spengler, Oswald 81
Stasiulis, Daiva 52
Stern, Fritz 17, 90
Stravinsky, Igor 43
structural racism 67
suicide bombers 60
Sweden Democrats 128
Swedish language 10
Sydsvenskan 28

Taylor, Charles 88, 90
Townsend, Peter 85
transferred nationalism 4, 22
Turnbull, Colin 20

unfair allegations 111–112
utopianism 82

vice of difference 27–37
Vilks, Lars 39, 40, 42, 79, 122
violence 5, 59, 61, 62, 64–66, 80, 82, 84–86, 123, 125
virtue of amnesia 27–37
virulent nationalism 117–118

war-time paraphernalia 16
Webster, Yehudi O. 24, 25, 105, 106
Weidenholzer, Joseph 38, 39, 41–42, 44
Weill, Kurt 45
West, Jonathan 23
West, Patrick 12, 87, 91
white trash 110–111
women 1, 65, 73–75, 80, 116
workers 53, 94, 95, 97, 111

xenophobes 112

Printed in the United States
By Bookmasters